EPHESIANS
A SELF-STUDY GUIDE

Irving L. Jensen

MOODY PRESS
CHICAGO

© 1973 by
THE MOODY BIBLE INSTITUTE
OF CHICAGO

Moody Press Revised Edition, 1990

Scripture quotations, unless noted otherwise, are taken from the King James Version

The use of selected references from various versions of the Bible in this publication does not necessarily imply publisher endorsement of the versions in their entirety

ISBN 0-8024-4454-7

7 9 10 8 6

Printed in the United States of America

Contents

Introduction

The average Christian is not fully aware of all the inheritance that is his in Christ. Nor does he know the extent of the spiritual power offered to him daily by God to help him live a full and vibrant Christian life. These are some of the reasons that God included Paul's letter to the Ephesians in His holy Scriptures. The epistle has been an inspiration to new Christians as well as to veterans in the household of God. It is always contemporary, ever fresh and challenging. As you launch into your study of Ephesians, you may rightly expect to learn from God new and wonderful things that *He wrote for you.*

Beginning with Lesson 3, there are six main parts to each lesson:

1. *Preparing for study.* Here you are helped to get started in your study of the passage by looking at backgrounds of the text, reviewing the previous lesson, and viewing the overall context of the passage. Momentum is a key to progress in study, and it is important to get such momentum early in your study.

2. *Analysis.* This is the key part of the lesson. Here you analyze the text of the Bible (paragraphs, sentences, words). Emphasis is on independent Bible study—seeing for yourself what the Bible says. You are constantly urged to (1) *look* and (2) *record* what you see. The analytical chart method is used from time to time for analysis of the passage (e.g., Chart J). Included in this section of the lesson are many questions that are intended to encourage searching and digging.

3. *Notes.* These are comments on items singled out in the lesson for which the text itself does not give complete information (e.g., biographical background) or for which the meaning is not clear.

4. *For thought and discussion.* This is the practical section of the lesson. Questions and suggestions are given to help you apply

4

the Bible text to daily life. Spend time reflecting on what the Bible says and means. "Contemplation is the channel from the head to the heart." If you are studying in a group you will want to discuss these various subjects.

5. *Further study.* Subjects for extended study are suggested here. Continuity in the study manual is not broken, however, if this section is passed over at this time. You may want to return to these studies at a later date.

6. *Words to ponder.* "Meditation lights the match to the logs." Usually a short verse is cited here for meditation. As you conclude each lesson pray that God will help you apply the truths you learned.

Suggestions for Using This Manual

1. There are ten lessons in this manual. You may want to study some of the lessons in two or more units because of the length of the passage involved. Undertake only what you can study without the pressure of limited time.

2. There are three basic tools for study: a good edition of the Bible, paper, and a pencil. Your Bible should have space in its margins for notations. (The King James Version is the basic version used in this self-study series.)

3. Develop personal study habits that are suited to your own abilities and inclinations. The following elements are basic to effective study, whatever the method:

a) Schedule. Set aside *time*; set aside a *regular* time.

b) Desire. Guard this with all your strength.

c) Methodicalness. Avoid dabbling in a haphazard fashion. Be orderly. Learn and apply different methods suggested.

d) Recording. Keep your pencil busy. This is a main emphasis in this self-study series. "The pencil is one of the best eyes."

e) Dependence. Look to the Spirit's enlightenment for help in seeing, interpreting, and applying the Bible text.

4. The following outside helps will facilitate your study:

a) One or two good modern Bible versions, for purposes of comparison. Analytical Bible study should *concentrate on* one version of the Bible and *compare* readings of other translations or paraphrases. Such comparative study throws light on obscure passages, extends the scope of vision, and excites overall interest in the passage being studied. (Keep in mind the difference between a *translation* and a *paraphrase.* A translation translates the original Bible text word for word as much as possible, without amplifying or interpreting in any way. A paraphrase takes the liberty of giving the sense of the Bible text without being confined to a strict word economy. An example of a translation is the *New American Standard Bible*; an example of a paraphrase is *The Living Bible*.)

    b) A Bible dictionary or encyclopedia
    c) An exhaustive concordance
    d) A commentary for help on difficult passages
    e) A book on word studies

Suggestions for Group Leaders

1. Make clear to the members of the class what you want them to do in preparation for the next meeting. Encourage them to use a notebook, writing out answers to all questions and recording observations on the analytical charts when these are called for.

2. Stimulate discussion during the class meeting. Encourage everyone to participate. Let the Bible speak to contemporary problems.

3. Encourage the members to ask questions about difficult verses. Recognize problem passages in the Bible when they appear. Don't hesitate to say, "I don't know," when this is so. It will increase the group's respect for you. Use such occasions to emphasize the maxim of interpretation that whatever is essential in the Bible is clear.

4. Use the eye gate as much as possible in your group meetings. If possible reproduce on a chalkboard the main charts of the manual. If you have access to an overhead projector, this can be very effective.

5. Devote the last part of your meeting to sharing the spiritual lessons taught by the Scripture passage. This should be the climax of the class hour.

6. Close the meeting on time, just as you opened on time. Further discussion with members who have questions or problems can be continued after the meeting has been officially concluded.

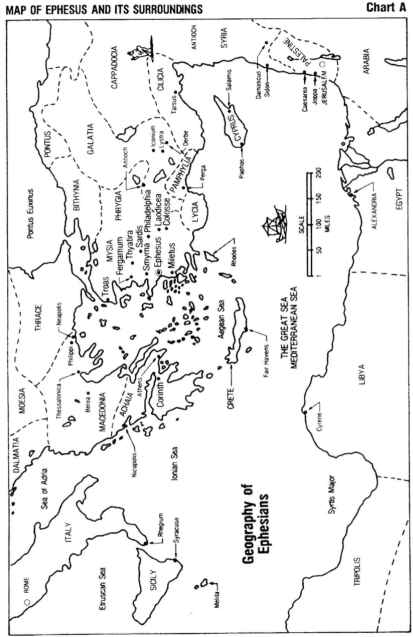

Geography of
Ephesians

Lesson 1
Background of Ephesians

The profound message of Ephesians was originally sent to Christians who had been saved only a few years. Read Acts 19:17-20 for one glimpse of this group before and after their conversion (A.D.55). Little did the Christians know then that the bonfire of their heathen books, worth more than ten thousand dollars, would bring forth out of its ashes a spiritual gold mine—one short book of Ephesians—just six years later.

In this lesson we will want to study the background of Paul's letter to the Ephesians to help us better appreciate and understand the message of the Bible text. This follows the usual order of study, which is: (1) viewing the background, (2) surveying the whole book, (3) analyzing the parts.

1. AUTHOR

Twice in the text of Ephesians, Paul is identified as the author. Read 1:1 and 3:1. Internal evidences of style and context, as well as the external witness of tradition, support this observation.

Paul was around sixty-five years of age when he wrote the letter. He referred to himself as an "aged man" when he wrote to Philemon at this same time.

If you have not recently studied the life and ministry of this great apostle, you may want to refer to a brief treatment of Paul's biography in a Bible dictionary or encyclopedia.

II. DESTINATION

A. Main Views

There are two views as to the original destination of Paul's letter:

1. *The church of Ephesus*. This view is supported by the reading of 1:1 and by the traditional title assigned the epistle by the early church Fathers: "To Ephesians" (Greek, *pros Ephesious*). Also, such verses as 4:17 and 6:21-22 point to a *specific* church as being addressed, whatever that church was.

2. *A circuit of various unspecified churches*. This view is based mainly on the fact that some important ancient manuscripts omit the phrase "at Ephesus" (Greek, *en epheso*) in 1:1.[1] Also, the epistle as a whole lacks the usual Pauline personal greetings and so appears to be a circular letter.[2]

Each of the above views has its strengths and weaknesses. Perhaps the answer is found in combining the two views. In the words of one writer, "The epistle was written to the Ephesians and addressed to them, but . . . the Apostle intentionally cast it into a form which would make it suitable to the Christians in the neighboring churches and intended that it should be communicated to them."[3]

See Chart A ("Geography of Ephesians") for the location of churches in the vicinity of Ephesus who would have read Paul's letter sooner or later. Compare these with the locations of the churches to whom John sent Revelation (Rev. 1:11). Read Acts 19:8-10; 20:31 for reference to Paul's three-year ministry to people living in Ephesus and the regions round about.

B. The City of Ephesus

The Christians living in and around Ephesus to whom Paul wrote this sublime epistle were cosmopolitan-oriented and well informed about world affairs. This was because of the city's strategic location. Ephesus was recognized as the "first" city of the province of Asia, even though Pergamum, ninety miles to the north, was its capital. Try to imagine some of the native characteristics of the congregation at Ephesus from these brief notes about the city:

1. *Commerce*. Ephesus was one of the three leaders of international trade, the other two being Alexandria of Egypt and Antioch of Syria. Note on Chart A the city's trade-oriented location.

2. *Arts and sciences*. The city was a haven for philosophers, poets, artists, and orators. Corinth, across the Aegean Sea, was one of its rivals in those disciplines.

1 Main examples are the two primary uncials, Sinaiticus and Vaticanus (4th century), and the Chester Beatty papyri (3d century)
2. An exception is 6:21.
3. D. Edmond Hiebert, *An Introduction to the Pauline Epistles*, p 266.

3. *Religion.* The worship of Diana (Artemis) was the dominant religion of this area. The Temple of Diana was world famous. Read Acts 19:23-34, noting among other things that Demetrius boasted that "all Asia and the world" worshiped Diana (19:27). Many of the Ephesians also identified with the imperial cult of Augustus and with various forms of magic (cf. Acts 19:13-19; Eph. 6:12). When you study Ephesians, try to recall from time to time that its original readers were converts from the darkness of these idolatries.

C. The Church of Ephesus

Read the following passages for what they reveal concerning the Ephesian church. Look for such things as first converts, leaders, and organizational growth. Record your findings.

1. *Pentecost converts from Asia*
A.D. 30—Acts 2:9

---

2. Before Paul's extended campaign at Ephesus
A.D. 52—Acts 18:18-21

18:24-26

---

3. *During the extended campaign*
A.D. 52-56—Acts 19

Acts 20:17-27 (Paul recalling the past)

---

4. *Charge to the Ephesian elders*
A.D. 55-56—Acts 20:28-38

---

5. *Charge to Timothy*
A.D. 64—1 Timothy 1:3

Most of the Ephesian congregation were Gentile converts, though the number of Jewish Christians was not small. Note the two references to "Jews and Greeks" in Acts 19:10, 17. Since their conversion took place in A.D. 55, and Ephesians was written in A.D. 61, the congregation was relatively young in the Lord when they read Paul's letter for the first time. The church itself served as a

10

"mother church" to the others of the province. By the time the apostle John became a spiritual shepherd of the Asian Christians toward the end of the first century, the Ephesian church was regarded as the headquarters of Christian missions, succeeding Antioch of Syria (which had succeeded Jerusalem). Observe in Revelation 1:11 the location of the name *Ephesus* in the list of the seven churches. Does this suggest something to you?

III. DATE AND PLACE WRITTEN

A date assigned to the writing of Ephesians is A.D. 61. This is based on Paul's writing the epistle during his first imprisonment in Rome, which lasted at least two years (A.D. 61-62). At this time he also wrote Colossians, Philemon, and Philippians. The four are generally referred to as the prison epistles. Read Acts 28:30-31. Were circumstances favorable to Paul to meditate, study, and write

CHRONOLOGICAL ORDER OF THE PAULINE EPISTLES   **Chart B**

MISSIONARY TOURS	FIRST IMPRISONMENT	RELEASE	FINAL IMPRISONMENT
A.D. 48-56	61-62	62-67	67
GALATIANS between tours 1 and 2			
- - - - - - - -	COLOSSIANS PHILEMON EPHESIANS	1 TIMOTHY	2 TIMOTHY
1 THESSALONIANS 2 THESSALONIANS		- - - - - - -	
tour 2	- - - - - - -	TITUS	
- - - - - - -	PHILIPPIANS		
1 CORINTHIANS 2 CORINTHIANS ROMANS tour 3			
6 EPISTLES	4 EPISTLES	2 EPISTLES	1 EPISTLE

11

during this imprisonment? John Bunyan wrote the classic *Pilgrim's Progress* while in prison. Have you read of other "prison masterpieces"? How do you account for such a phenomenon?

Chart B shows the four periods of Paul's public ministry during which he wrote epistles. Each list of books is shown in the chronological order of writing.[4] Colossians, Ephesians, and Philemon are grouped together, since these were written and dispatched at the same time by the same messengers (read Eph. 6:21-22; Col. 4:7-9; Philem. 12).

For Paul's references in the prison epistles to his imprisonment, read the following passages in the four epistles: Colossians 4:3, 18; Ephesians 3:1; 4:1; 6:20; Philemon 10, 13, (23); and Philippians 1:7, 13.

Also read the following verses, which indicate Paul was expecting release from his first imprisonment in Rome: Philippians 1:19-26 and Philemon 22.

IV. OCCASION AND PURPOSE OF THE EPISTLE

Ephesians does not give a clue to any specific problem in the Ephesian church to which the epistle may have been directed. By "specific problem" is meant such things as heresy (e.g., Colossians); internal strife (1 Corinthians); false accusations (2 Corinthians); false doctrine (Galatians). But when Paul wrote Ephesians he must have still been thinking of such evils as doctrinal heresy threatening the neighboring church at Colosse, which he specifically referred to in his letter to the Colossians. No church is ever immune to doctrinal defilement, so it could be that the apostle's positive teachings in Ephesus on the pure knowledge of Christ were directed to the same kinds of problems vexing the Colossian church. Also, the Christians at Colosse would eventually be reading Ephesians, as it made the rounds of the churches of Asia. Hiebert writes on this:

> Judging from its close relation to Colossians, it appears that the conflict which caused the writing of Colossians likewise called forth this epistle. The Colossian conflict revealed to Paul the need for a fuller statement of God's program for the universe as it centers in Christ in His relationship to the church[5]

No doubt there were individual problems in the Ephesian church. But the basic need of the young Christians there was to

4 Authorities differ in assigning dates to some of Paul's epistles. Hebrews, an anonymous letter, is not included in this list.
5. Hiebert, p. 266.

grow spiritually in the Lord, by (1) an increasing awareness of their relationship to Him and His ministry to them through the Spirit and (2) the day-to-day experience of walking in that light. Paul was inspired to address this epistle to that basic need. And it can be said without qualification that now almost two thousand years later the letter still serves the same function for the children of God.

V. CONTENTS

Much of our survey study of Lesson 2 will concentrate on the contents of Ephesians, especially *main* contents. A preview of some of those things is given below.

A. Doctrine

1. Salvation: as a deliverance *from* and deliverance *unto*
2. Union with Christ: an inscrutable yet real relationship
3. The church universal: as the Body of Christ, who is its Head
4. Holy Spirit: the source of every blessing and power in the Christian life
5. Will and work of God: for man's benefit and God's glory

B. Prayer and Praise

Two notable prayers appear at 1:15-23 and 3:14-21. The opening passage 1:3-14 has been called a "Hymn of Grace." The epistle has been well described as one of "instruction passing into prayer, a creed soaring into an impassioned psalm."

C. Practice

At least half the epistle is devoted to the practical walk of the believer in Christ. The Christian's *walking* (4:1) and *standing* (6:11) are based on his *sitting* (2:6). His life in Christ (chaps. 4-6) is drawn from his heritage in Christ (chaps. 1-3). The armor passage of 6:10-17 is a classic Scripture portion describing the weaponry of the Christian's spiritual warfare.

D. General Characteristics

Ephesians is a book of superlatives. It is the sublimest of all of Paul's epistles, for which it has been called "The Grand Canyon of Scripture." There are very few personal notes and biographical references, and, as noted earlier, controversies and problems are not discussed here. Paul is not ignoring the practical mundane issues, as though they were unimportant. (It has already been noted that at least half of the epistle is practical in purpose.) Rather, the apostle has a vision of the heavenly realm, and in the quiet and calm of his imprisonment he is inspired by the Spirit to share this with his readers.[6] Philip Schaff describes this aspect of the epistle:

> It certainly is the most spiritual and devout, composed in an exalted and transcendent state of mind, where theology rises into worship and meditation into oration. It is the Epistle of the Heavenlies. . The aged apostle soared high above all earthly things to the invisible and eternal realities in heaven. From his gloomy confinement he ascended for a season to the mount of transfiguration. The prisoner of Christ, chained to a pagan soldier, was transformed into a conqueror, clad in the panoply of God, and singing a paean of victory.[7]

The distinctive language and style of Ephesians reflects the richness and depth of its message. Someone has observed that the letter contains forty-two words (e.g., "obtained an inheritance," 1:11) not found in any other New Testament book, and forty-three not used by Paul in his other writings. One of the prominent features of Paul's style in Ephesians is its long sentences, described thus by one writer: "The sentences flow on as it were in the full strong tide, wave after wave, of an immense and impetuous sea, swayed by a powerful wind, and brightened and sparkling with the golden rays of a rising sun." This suggests something of the excitement and inspiration in store for you as you move into the analytical studies of the Bible text. As one Bible student has well said, "If we persevere with our study of Paul, we shall soon discover that we are sitting at the feet of one who, more than any other human being, has got 'far ben [within]' into the wonders and the glories of that 'open secret of God' which is 'Christ in you, the hope of glory' (Col. ii. 2 and i. 27)."[8]

VI. RELATION TO OTHER NEW TESTAMENT BOOKS

A. Prison Epistles

We have already seen that the four prison epistles—Ephe-

---

6 The word *heaven(s)* appears four times, and *heavenly places* (or *heavenlies)* four times, in Ephesians.

7. Philip Schaff, *History of the Christian Church* (New York: Scribner, 1910), 1·780

8. Alexander Ross, "The Pauline Epistles," in *The New Bible Commentary*, p 69.

sians, Philippians, Colossians, and Philemon—were written about the same time. This would account for at least some of the similarities of these books. Ephesians, Philippians, and Colossians were written to local churches of those cities; Philemon, although written particularly to a personal friend of Paul, was also addressed to the church meeting in Philemon's house (Philem. 2; cf. Col. 4:15).

B. Ephesians and Colossians

Ephesians and Colossians have been called twin epistles because of their many likenesses. Phrases of 78 of the 155 verses in Ephesians are very similar to phrases in Colossians. This is explained by the fact that both epistles were written with the same general purpose: to show the relationship between Christ and His church as assurance and correction to young Christians growing in the Lord.

But the two epistles are far from being *identical* twins. Some differences are shown in Chart C.

COLOSSIANS AND EPHESIANS COMPARED   Chart C

COLOSSIANS	EPHESIANS
CHRIST AND THE COSMOS	CHRIST AND THE CHURCH
Emphasis on Christ Head of the Church	Emphasis on the Church Body of Christ
MORE PERSONAL; LOCAL	LESS PERSONAL; LOFTY
COMBATS ERROR DIRECTLY	COMBATS ERROR INDIRECTLY
TONE: intensity and tumult of a battlefield	TONE: calmness of surveying the field after victory

C. Galatians, Ephesians, and Philippians

Chart D shows some comparisons of these Pauline letters.

15

	GALATIANS	EPHESIANS	PHILIPPIANS
STYLE	mainly logical and argumentative	doctrinal and hortatory	informative and consoling
A MAIN SUBJECT	SALVATION	CHRIST	LIFE OF JOY
PURPOSE	CORRECTIVE	INSTRUCTIVE	INSPIRATIONAL
TONE	sharp, rebuking	calm, victorious	tender, joyful

VII. A STUDY EXERCISE

Here is a study exercise that will show you things that were especially on Paul's mind when he wrote Colossians and Ephesians. The references below show parallel passages in these two epistles where similar or identical phrases appear. These things that Paul wrote in Colossians and repeated soon thereafter in Ephesians will be clues to us as to what things were prominent in his thinking at that time. Read each set, and record the similar phrases.

VIII. SOME REVIEW QUESTIONS

1. How old was Paul when he wrote Ephesians? Where was he when he composed the letter?

2. What are the two main views as to whom Ephesians was originally sent? What are your conclusions?

3. How would you describe the average member of the church at Ephesus in the year A.D. 61?

4. Reconstruct the story of how the Ephesians were first saved and how the local church came to be organized.

Ephesians	Colossians
1:1-2	1:1-2
1:4	1.22
1:7	1:14
1:10	1:20
1:15-17	1:3-4
1:18	1:17
1:21-23	1:16, 18-19
2:1, 2, 12	1:21
2:15	2:14
2:16	1:20, 22
3:1-3	1:24-26
3:7-9	1:23, 25, 27-28
4:1	1:10
4:2-4	3:12-15
4:16	2:19
4:22-24	3:9-10
4:25-26	3:8-9
4:29	3:8; 4·6
4:31	3:8
4:32	3:12-13
5:3-6	3:5-8
5:15	4:5
5:19-22	3:16-18
5:25	3:19
6:1-4	3:20-21
6:5-9	3:22—4:1
6:19-20	4:3-4
6:21-22	4:7-8

5. Do you think the message of Ephesians was too deep for the young converts at Ephesus? Who should be reading and studying Ephesians today?

6. What relationship was there between the church at Ephesus and churches in surrounding cities (e.g., Colosse)?

7. What were some of Paul's reasons for writing this letter to the churches of Asia?

8. What are some of the main doctrines taught in Ephesians?

9. Identify some of the letter's characteristics, such as style and tone.

10. Compare Ephesians and Colossians. How do you account for the many likenesses?

11. From what you have learned thus far in your study of Ephesians, how can this epistle help Christians today?

IX. PREPARE FOR THE NEXT LESSON

Beginning with the next lesson you will be studying the *Bible text itself*. Are you expecting anything from God as a fruit of your studies? Are you willing to devote time and concentration to this challenging project? Reflect on this experience of a teenage youth, John A. Mackay, who became one of the great Scottish-American theologians:

> I can never forget that the reading of this Pauline letter, when I was a boy in my teens, exercised a more decisive influence upon my thought and imagination than was ever wrought upon me before or since by the perusal of any piece of literature .. I have to admit, without shame or reserve, that, as a result of that encounter, I have been unable to think of my own life or the life of mankind or the life of the cosmos apart from Jesus Christ [9]

9. Testimony in part quoted by F.F. Bruce, *The Epistle to the Ephesians,* p 16

Lesson 2
Survey of Ephesians

With this lesson we begin our study of the actual text of Paul's letter to the Ephesians. Our task here is to survey the book as a whole, to see its *general* makeup. Analysis of smaller individual parts begins in Lesson 3. This procedure follows the standard rule, "Image the whole (survey), then execute the parts (analysis)."

James M. Gray, former president of Moody Bible Institute, was first introduced to the survey (or synthetic) method of Bible study in an interesting way. S. Maxwell Coder tells the story:

> As a pastor, Dr. Gray longed to know the Word better. One day he observed in a layman a spiritual poise to which he himself was something of a stranger Asked the secret of his joy and peace, the layman said that he had found it by reading Ephesians. On a Sunday afternoon he had read the epistle through once while lying under a tree. His interest aroused, he read it through again and again.
>
> After the twelfth reading, he said, "I was in possession of the epistle to the Ephesians or, better yet, it was in possession of me, and I came to understand what it meant for Christian believers to be 'seated together in heavenly places in Christ Jesus,' in a sense in which I had never understood it before, and in a sense in which the meaning and, I trust, the power and joy of it will never depart from me while I live."
>
> At once Dr. Gray began to follow the method. It was so simple that he could not understand why he had not discovered it sooner. Instead of reading the Bible straight through or selected parts of it, he read and re-read each book until it became a part of him.[1]

1. S Maxwell Coder, "Three Good Methods of Bible Study," *Moody Monthly*, Feb. 1958, p 19

The self-study guides of this series follow this basic approach to the Scriptures that Dr. Gray learned: Study the Bible the way God wrote it, namely, *book by book.*

Your survey study of Ephesians will be both stimulating and fruitful if you know *what* you are searching for and *how* to do the searching. Four main activities constitute the *what* of survey study:

1. Discovering the book's overall *theme*

2. Observing *patterns* and *movements* in the structure (organization) of the book

3. Noting *highlights* of the book and finding *clues* for the study of its various parts

4. Getting a feel of the book's *atmosphere* and approach

Keep these goals always before you as you make your survey of Ephesians.

As to the *how* (method) of survey study, there are various orders of procedure. Basically, however, survey study is of three main stages: (1) making the initial acquaintance of the book, (2) scanning the prominent individual items, and (3) seeing how the parts are put together. These are the things we will be doing for the remainder of this lesson. An important bit of advice here is that throughout your survey study you avoid getting bogged down in details. Keep in mind that detailed analysis begins with Lesson 3.

I. THE FIRST READING

1. Scan the letter of Ephesians in one sitting. You may choose to do this first in a modern version and then in the version of your basic study. In this initial reading you should overlook such things as chapter divisions. James Gray advises:

> Read continuously, at a single sitting, disregarding the divisions into chapters and verses. Reading straight through without interruption makes it possible to discover the central line of thought, the basic themes presented in the book under consideration. To read part of a book now and part of another time is to lose the thread. To interrupt one's reading by observing chapter divisions may mean missing the continuity of a theme developed over several chapters [2]

2. Write down your first impressions of the book.

3. What is the atmosphere of the book as a whole?

4. List a few key words and phrases that stand out as of this reading.

2 Quoted by Coder, p. 19.

II. SUBSEQUENT READINGS

1. Before reading the epistle again, mark in your Bible the paragraph divisions that are shown on Chart E. Make the markings clearly visible in your Bible, for you will be using them over and over. (Note: Each reference on the chart is the opening verse of the particular paragraph.)

2. Now read the letter paragraph by paragraph and record a *paragraph title* in each space on Chart E. (A paragraph title is a strong word or phrase taken from the text, intended to serve as a clue to at least one main part of the paragraph. Examples are shown.) This group of titles is not an outline of Ephesians. It is merely an indicator of prominent subjects.

PARAGRAPH TITLES   **Chart E**

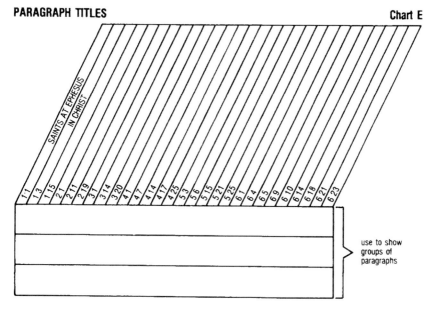

Doing this exercise helps you get initial momentum in survey study.

3. Is there an introduction and conclusion to the letter? What are the verses?

4. Did you notice any major turning point in the book? If so, where?

5. Add to the list of key words and phrases that you began earlier in this study.

6. Did you observe any personal references, such as names of people?

7. Where in Ephesians do prayers of Paul appear?

III. OBSERVING THE STRUCTURE OF THE EPISTLE

Now we will want to see how the various parts of Ephesians are related to each other. Two key things to look for in this structure study are (1) main turning points and (2) groupings of paragraphs.

A. Main Turning Points

You probably have already observed that there is a change in the epistle at the end of chapter 3. How is this supported by the following?
1. The content of 3:20-21

2. The last word of 3:21

3. The first two words of 4:1

4. The general content of chapters 4–6 as compared with 1–3 (for example, which chapters are predominantly practical?)

B. Groupings of Paragraphs

Some groups of paragraphs are not always easy to detect in the early stages of study. What subject appears in paragraph 5:21-24 that continues into the next paragraphs? Where then does a new general subject begin? Identify the group beginning at 5:21 with a title. Record this on Chart E. Try to identify other groups in the epistle.

How does paragraph 6:10-20 serve as a concluding paragraph to the epistle (not counting paragraph 6:21-24)?

C. The Survey Chart

There are various ways one may record a study of the structure of a Bible book. A survey chart (see Chart F) is one such way. One of the advantages of a survey chart over the conventional outline is that various topical outlines can be viewed simultaneously

EPHESIANS CHRIST AND THE CHURCH

PRAISE	PRAYER	KNOW 1:18	REMEMBER 2:11	FAINT NOT 3:13	WALK WORTHILY 4:1	PUT ON 6:11
1:3	1:15	BLESSINGS IN CHRIST	EXPERIENCE OF SALVATION	GROWING KNOWLEDGE AND STRENGTH	CHRISTIAN CONDUCT	CHRISTIAN ARMOR
INTRODUCTION		position and possessions	PAST without Christ / PRESENT with Christ	present and future	church unity / daily walk / domestic duty	THE CONFLICT
1:1		2:1	3:1 / 3:2	3:14 / 4:1	4:17 / 5:21 / 6:10	6:21 CONCLUSION

PARENTHESIS —PAUL'S TESTIMONY

EXHORTATION	TESTIMONY AND PRAYER	COMMANDS AND EXHORTATIONS
OUR HERITAGE IN CHRIST		OUR LIFE IN CHRIST
"I pray that you may know your resources in Christ"	Therefore →	"I pray that you may live consistent with your faith in Christ"
WE IN CHRIST (IN HIM 1 4)		CHRIST IN US (IN US) (cf 3.20)
WORK OF GOD		WALK OF THE CHRISTIAN
heavenly standing		earthly walk

—every blessing / —sealing	—access / —growth	—power / —revelation	—unity / —holiness	—joy / —thanksgiving	—prayer / —word

HOLY SPIRIT

Key Verses
2 19-20
1 22-23

Key Words
church
in Christ
in Him
heavenly places
according to
power
riches
glory
one
love
walk
even as
grace
spiritual
Spirit
mystery

23

for comparative purposes. Also, a survey chart is a vivid eye-gate reference for context as one analyzes a small part of the book. We will refer to this chart often during our analytical studies.

You may want to construct your own survey chart, recording observations you have already made. In any case, study Chart F very carefully before proceeding with the next lesson, for such an overview of Ephesians will help you immeasurably as you proceed with your analytical studies.

Observe the following on Chart F:

1. Ephesians is divided into two main parts. Which is mainly doctrinal, and which is mainly practical?

2. "Our Heritage in Christ" is related to "Our Life in Christ" by the word "therefore" (see 4:1). What is the practical lesson suggested by this?

3. Note the two sections WE IN CHRIST and CHRIST IN US. Scan chapter 1 for the many appearances of the phrase "in him" (and similar phrases). Then read 3:20 (cf. 3:17) for the phrase "worketh in us," which anticipates the development of the theme CHRIST IN US in the chapters to come.

4. The passage 3:2-13 is shown as a parenthesis in chapter 3. Read the chapter and observe why 3:2-13 is parenthetical.

5. Observe the commands shown at the top of the chart (e.g., KNOW). Read each verse in the Bible text. Relate the command words to the outlines shown below them on the chart. Compare these outlines with your own studies made thus far.

IV. FINAL OBSERVATIONS AND CONCLUSIONS

1. *Main theme.* In your own words, what is the main theme of Ephesians?

2. *Title.* Assign a title to Ephesians to coincide with its main theme. Note the one given on Chart F.

3. *A key verse.* Look for a verse in the letter that represents its theme. You may find more than one.

4. *Key words.* There are many key words in Ephesians. If you had to limit the list to ten, which ones would you choose?

5. *Classic passages.* Here are five passages that are often quoted or memorized: 1:17-23; 2:4-10; 2:19-22; 3:14-21; 6:10-17. Identify the main point of each.

V. TOPICAL STUDIES

At various times in the course of your study of Ephesians you may want to make an extended study of different subjects that appear throughout the epistle. Topics suggested for such study are listed below:

1. Paul as seen in the epistle (for example, see 3:1, 8, 13; 6:19-20)

2. The Ephesian Christians as seen in the epistle (see 1:15; 2:11; 3:13; 4:1ff.; 6:10ff)

3. God the Father

4. God the Son

5. God the Holy Spirit (see the outline on Chart F)

6. The "heavenlies"

7. The subjects of faith, hope, love, prayer, power

8. Eternity

Lesson 3

Ephesians 1:1-14

Spiritual Blessings in Christ

Paul gets to the heart of his message without preliminaries or delay in his Ephesian letter. After an unusually brief salutation, the reader is quickly caught up with the apostle into the realm of the heavenlies. The passage of this lesson is one of the sublime portions of the epistle, and yet its mysteries are not hidden from the understanding of God's children. In this connection we may remind ourselves that the great doctrines of the Bible are described by the writers in human language so that we may understand them better. How else can one explain why God used everyday words such as "chosen," "adoption," "redemption," "inheritance," and "sealed" (Eph. 1) to teach the sublime truths of eternal salvation?

I. PREPARATION FOR STUDY

We have already observed that the title of this lesson is "Spiritual Blessings in Christ." This is taken from 1:3 (read the verse). Such a subject is not very popular in times of affluence when materialism is the religion of most people. Christian workers are constantly pressured to make the gospel tangible—something that can be transacted across the counter and deposited in a safety vault. But the answer must always be that the gospel is not a commodity but a Person and that its message is a spiritual message about spiritual life, a new life brought into fellowship with God, who is Spirit. The physical must be involved, for the *whole* of man is saved in regeneration, but the spiritual is the underlying, determinative experience.

At the outset of our study of Ephesians we should ask and answer some questions about this word *spiritual* so that we will appreciate and understand why Paul has so much to say about this aspect of our life. The questions given below are not questions

about the passage of this lesson. Rather they are introductory
questions to prepare us for our study of Ephesians.
1. What does the word *spiritual* mean to you? What part of you is
spirit (cf. 1 Thess. 5:23)?

_____

_____

Read the following selected verses of the New Testament where
the word *spiritual* appears: Ephesians 5:19; Colossians 1:9; 3:16; 1
Peter 2:5; 1 Corinthians 2:14-15; 3:1; 9:11; Galatians 6:1; Romans
8:6.
What is the Holy Spirit's relation to the spirit of a believer?

_____

2. Can the word *spiritual* be applied to the evil world? If so, in
what sense (cf. Eph. 6:12)?

_____

_____

3. Is your spirit just as real as your flesh, which you can touch?
Give reasons for your answer.

_____

_____

_____

4. How much of the activities of your spirit is represented by these
three words: intellect, emotion, will?

_____

_____

_____

5. Do the above three activities have any bearing on what you do
in a physical way? If so, what, and how?

_____

_____

_____

6. Can you talk with God? In what realm? (Read John 4:24).

_____

_____

7. How would you compare spiritual wealth and material wealth?

_____

_____

8. In the light of your answers to the preceding questions, how would you define and describe "spiritual blessings?"

_____

_____

CONTEXT OF 1:1-14   **Chart G**

SALUTATION	BLESSINGS IN CHRIST	
	Position and Possessions	
	"I pray that you may know your resources in Christ" ➡	
	PRAISE	PRAYER
1:1	1:3	1:15 1:23

THIS LESSON

Refer to the survey Chart F, and observe the part 1:1-14 plays in the overall plan of the epistle. Chart G is an excerpt from that survey. The shaded area is the passage of this lesson.
"Launch out into the deep." Read Luke 5:4 where this interesting phrase appears. Read also the verses 5-9b, which record the successful results of the fishing venture of Jesus' disciples. What was the secret to success?

_____

_____

Apply this story to your project of studying Ephesians. What attitude and approach will ensure "a great multitude of fishes"?

_____

_____

II. ANALYSIS

Segment to be analyzed: 1:1-14
Paragraph divisions: at verses 1, 3

A. Salutation: 1:1-2

1. Read the salutation once, then read various salutations of Paul in other epistles. What are some likenesses and differences?

_____

_____

_____

2. Read the Ephesians' salutation again. What three different words does Paul use here to identify Christians (including himself)? What important aspect of the Christian life is represented by each word?

a) _____

b) _____

c) _____

What references are made to God and to Jesus? How does Paul use these phrases (note the different prepositions):
a) "of Jesus Christ":

_____

b) "in Christ Jesus":

_____

c) "from the Lord Jesus Christ":

_____

What do the different names and titles of God's Son suggest to you (e.g., read Matt. 1:21)?

_____

3. What are "grace" and "peace?" How are the two related in the salutation? Why is the order not given as "peace and grace"?

_____

_____

_____

B. Hymn of Praise: 1:3-14

1. The Paragraph as a Whole
a) First read this passage through without pausing. What are your impressions? If you are using a King James Version, you cannot help but observe how long the sentences are. In fact, how many sentences are there in the entire paragraph? We will study all twelve verses as one paragraph since the multitude of phrases seem to be all blended into one grand chord of praise. One writer calls the passage "a kaleidoscope of dazzling lights and shifting colours." Paul here was not thinking of grammar as he wrote. "The mighty surge of apostolic thought and inspiration sweeps over the narrow confines of rigid grammatical analysis."[1]
b) Read the passage again and underline in your Bible the references to praise. Is the word "blessed" (1:3) a praise word?
c) Read the paragraph again, this time underlining in your Bible the key phrase "in Christ" (and similar phrases, such as "in him"). Would it be correct to conclude that this phrase is the central *core* of the passage?
Verse 3 introduces the general theme of the paragraph: "spiritual blessings . . . in Christ." Note how often the root "bless" appears in the verse.
For what kind of blessings should a Christian be thankful?

How does the phrase "in heavenly places" describe them?

Do Christians enjoy *temporal* blessings from the hand of God? Are temporal blessings and spiritual blessings related? If so, how? Compare Deuteronomy 28:1-6.

d) Now we will proceed to record on paper the various spiritual blessings that Paul cites in verses 4-14. Use Chart H to record these observations. (You may want to use a separate larger sheet of paper, laid out similar to Chart H.) The three main columns to be completed on the chart are titled Blessings in Christ: "accord-

1 Alexander Ross, "The Pauline Epistles," in *The New Bible Commentary*, p 1016

"Blessed be God ... who hath blessed us with all **SPIRITUAL BLESSINGS ... IN CHRIST**" (1:3).
STUDIES IN 1:4-14.

Chart H

OUTLINE OF BLESSINGS	VERSE	Blessings in Christ (underline the blessing, circle "in him," etc.)	"According to"	Practical Purposes
CHOSEN	4	chosen us (in him) before the foundation of the world		that we should be holy and without blame before him in love
PREDESTINED	5-6a		according to the good pleasure of his will	
GRACIOUSLY FAVORED	6b			
REDEEMED	7-8			
ALL THINGS GATHERED TOGETHER	9-10			
GIVEN (OR MADE) AN INHERITANCE	11-13a			
SEALED	13b-14			

31

ing to," and Practical Purposes. (Note that v. 3 is shown as the introduction to the passage.)

Go through the paragraph and observe what the Christian has been given because he is *in Christ*. Record each phrase on Chart H. An example is shown (*"chosen us* in him"). At this point in your study don't tarry over the *meaning* of the blessing. We will be working with that later.

Another key phrase in the passage is "according to." This phrase serves as a measuring stick to give the spiritual dimensions of the blessings being described. Record each occurrence of the phrase, including the words that follow it. (An example is shown. Not every box on the chart will have an entry.) Who is the one referred to—the Father or the Son—in each context of this repeated phrase?

A natural question to ask concerning these spiritual blessings is, "What are some of their practical purposes?" Paul doesn't give a full answer now, for he has in mind devoting the last half of the letter to that very subject. But he writes a few things here on this, introduced by such purpose words as "that," "to," and "unto." Identify these purpose clauses in the passage, and record them in the right-hand column. (An example of this is also given.) What purposes are repeated here?

e) How does the following outline represent this paragraph, in light of your study so far?

> Salvation: The Father planned it (1:4-6)
> Salvation: The Son paid for it (1:7-12)
> Salvation: The Spirit applied it (1:13-14)

2. The Paragraph Verse by Verse

Now that we have an overall view of this hymn of praise, we will want to focus on the details, such as clauses and words within the verses.

a) Chosen in Christ (1:4). Compare Mark 13:20, where the one Greek root is translated by the two words "elect" and "chosen." In what sense did God choose Christians before the foundation of the world?

What does this reveal about God?

32

What does it reveal about Christians?

_____

What does the phrase "holy and without blame" mean? Is it possible for a Christian to be this? If so, how? Compare Jude 24.

_____

_____

Some Bible versions read the phrase "in love" as part of the next thought, thus: "In love He predestined us."[2] Here is a paraphrase that keeps the words as part of the thought of verse 4: "We who stand before him covered with his love" (*The Living Bible*).

b) *Predestined by Jesus Christ* (1:5-6a). The word "predestinated" in the King James Version usually appears as "predestined" or "foreordained" in our contemporary Bible versions. It refers to the same doctrine of election taught by the word "chosen" (1:4). Whose will determine predestination?

_____

Unto what is a person predestined? (On "adoption," see *Notes.*)

_____

What is the ultimate fruit of this divine election?

_____

What does each of these words say to you: praise, glory, grace? What is the glory of God's grace?

_____

_____

c) *Graciously favored in the beloved* (1:6b). Most Bible versions translate 1:6b as "which He freely bestowed on us in the beloved."

2. This is the reading of the *New American Standard Bible*. See also Alfred Martin, "The Epistle to the Ephesians," in *The Wycliffe Bible Commentary*, p 1303 The original Scriptures did not have punctuation marks, identifying such things as the beginning of a new sentence. The punctuation of all our Bible versions is outside the province of scriptural inspiration

Literally, the phrase reads "wherein he hath *be-graced* us in the beloved." What is the ground of all of God's favors shown to you?

_____

_____

d) Redeemed in Christ (1:7-8). A dictionary definition of *redemption* is "deliverance upon payment of a ransom." An Old Testament illustration of this is Israel's redemption (deliverance) from the bondage of Egypt. (E.g., note the word "redeem" in Ex. 6:6). To what is a sinner captive? (Cf. John 8:24; 2 Tim. 2:26; Gal. 3:22.)

_____

According to 1:7, what is the price of ransom? (Cf. Acts 20:28; 1 Cor. 6:20; 1 Pet. 1:18-19.)

_____

What is the blessed fruit of redemption?

_____

e) All things gathered together in Christ (1:9-10). Read verse 9 in a modern version. Most versions translate the last two words as "in him" (that is, in Christ), rather than "in himself" (God). What is the important teaching of this verse?

_____

How is verse 9 related to verse 10? What do you think Paul means by these phrases: "Dispensation [administration] of the fulness of times," and "all things" (1:10)?

_____

Compare the readings of versions for suggestions. What does this verse teach about world history and its relation to Christ? Compare John 1:3 and Colossians 1:16-20, noting the many references to "all things."

_____

_____

_____

f) Given (or made) an inheritance in Christ (1:11-13*a*). How much of these verses appeared early in the paragraph? What is the Christian's "inheritance" (1:11)?[3]

Compare "we . . . who first trusted in Christ" (v. 12) and "in whom ye also trusted" (v. 13). If Paul meant Jews when he wrote "we" (v. 12), whom did he mean by "ye" (v. 13)?

---

g) Sealed with the Holy Spirit (1:13*b*-14). Interpret these verses with the help of the translations shown on the right:
"after that ye believed"—"having believed"
"sealed"—"marked with the stamp of ownership"
"earnest"—"guarantee," "down payment," "pledge"
"until the redemption of the purchased possession"—"until the day when God completes the redemption of what He has paid for as His own"
Why is assurance of salvation such a precious possession of the believer?

Does assurance rule out obligation? (See 4:30.)

What are the concluding words of the hymn in verse 14? Compare this with the opening words (v. 3). Why should the spirit of praise be natural for a Christian? What can hinder such a spirit?

Why is Christ the key to all of God's graces to mankind?

What really is meant by the phrase "in Christ"?

---

3. Most Bible versions prefer the alternate reading of 1.11*a*, which is "being made a heritage." In what sense is the believer a heritage of God? R.D.H. Lenski translates the verse thus "We were assigned a lot as having been predestined" (*St. Paul's Epistle to the Ephesians*, p 376).

35

Is this different from "by Christ"? If so, how?

_____

_____

_____

III. NOTES

1. "Heavenly places" (1:3). The one Greek word is sometimes translated as "heavenlies." The term appears only in Ephesians (1:3, 20; 2:6; 3:10; 6:12).[4] Read each verse cited and evaluate this definition of heavenlies: "That realm of spiritual realities in which the great forces of good and evil wage their warfare; in which also Jesus Christ sits supreme and we representatively in Him."

2. "He hath chosen us" (1:4). *The Amplified Bible* correctly adds the idea "for Himself" to represent the middle voice in the Greek: "He chose us—actually picked us out for Himself as His own." Only precious, eternal fruit comes of such election.

3. "Adoption of children" (1:5) The *New American Standard Bible* correctly translates "adoption as sons." The word "adoption" appears five times in the Bible, only in Paul's letters: Romans 8:15, 23; 9:4; Galatians 4:5; Ephesians 1:5. Adoption is God's work of placing a child of His in the position of adult son, with all of its privileges and rights. New birth and adoption take place at the same time when a believer accepts Jesus Christ as his Saviour.

4. "Mystery of his will" (1:9). Such mystery is a secret, undiscoverable by human reason. Only divine revelation uncovers its meaning to man.

5. "Dispensation" (1:10). The Greek word so translated comes from two roots—house and law—and was used in a secular sense to mean the management or administration of someone's property. The first part of verse 10 reads thus in the *New American Standard Bible*: "with a view to an administration suitable to the fulness of the times."

6. "Fulness of times" (1:10). This is the end of time in world history. Alfred Martin writes, "Evidently the dispensation of the fulness of times is the final stewardship committed to men, which will bring the purposes of God to fruition in world history."[5]

7. "All things" (1:10). The phrase no doubt includes the whole creation (cf. John 1:3; Col. 1:16-20). *The Living Bible* sees the gathering together of verse 10 as referring only to believers:

4. The King James Version reads "high places" in 6 12
5. Martin, p. 1304.

"when the time is ripe he will gather us all together from wherever we are—in heaven or on earth—to be with him—in Christ, forever."

IV. FOR THOUGHT AND DISCUSSION

1. The first question and answer of the historic Westminster Shorter Catechism:

Question: "What is the chief end of man?"

Answer: "Man's chief end is to glorify God, and to enjoy Him forever."

Refer back to the text, where the phrase "praise of his glory" appears three times. What is meant by the glory of God? In what ways can man glorify God?

2. Think more about what is meant by the phrase "in Christ." If a believer is in active union with Christ, how should this be manifested in his daily walk? Why is the *positional* truth of being "in Christ" so vital?

3. If you are studying in a group, discuss the subject of sovereign election. Consider such areas as the following:

   a) Who the elected ones are
   b) What determines who are elected
   c) What the fruits of election are

4. Is it true that world history will culminate at one point and that the point will be a Person, Jesus Christ? Relate 1:10 to this. Does this mean that all the world will eventually be saved? Compare Philippians 2:9-11.

5. What do you think of when you read in the Bible that you as a Christian "have obtained an inheritance" (1:11)? What is striking about the fact that you "have been made a heritage" of God?

V. FURTHER STUDY

A suggested topic for extended study is the efficacy of Christ's blood. Various outside sources will give help in this. As a starter, use the following outline on what Christ's blood accomplishes:

It justifies (Rom. 5:9).
It redeems man to God (1 Pet. 1:18-19).
It brings forgiveness (Eph. 1:7).
It cleanses the conscience (Heb. 9:14).
It sanctifies (Heb. 13:12).
It gives victory over Satan (Rev. 12:11).
It is the door to God's throne room (Heb. 10:19).

VI. WORDS TO PONDER

The spirit's seal upon us means that God has already purchased us and that he guarantees to bring us to himself. This is just one more reason for us to praise our glorious God (1:14*b*, *The Living Bible*).

Prayer for
Spiritual Wisdom

The prayer of the passage of this lesson is closely related to the hymn studied in 1:3-14. That hymn was Paul's testimony of praise to God for the boundless spiritual blessings in Christ. The prayer of 1:15-23 is the apostle's intercession for saints, that they may know the extent of their blessings in Christ. So in 1:3-14 the appeal to the reader is for a heart of praise; in 1:15-23 the appeal is for a spirit of wisdom. The Christian who earnestly covets and cultivates both of these is the maturing Christian, growing daily in the grace and knowledge of Jesus Christ. As you begin your study of this lesson, let it be the desire of your heart to experience the very things Paul prayed for in behalf of his Christian friends at Ephesus.

CONTEXT OF 1:15-23   **Chart I**

WE IN CHRIST			
"Know" (1:18)		"Remember" (2:11)	"Faint not" (3:13)
BLESSINGS IN CHRIST		EXPERIENCE OF SALVATION	GROWING KNOWLEDGE AND STRENGTH
PRAISE	PRAYER	EXHORTATION	PRAYER AND TESTIMONY
1:1	1:15	2:1	3:1 3:21

THIS LESSON

39

I. PREPARATION FOR STUDY

1. How would you grade the Christian community today as to its attitude of praise to God and its perception of spiritual truth? What are some causes of deficiency in these areas? Where is a cure to be found, and what might that cure be?

2. Read Psalm 110 as background for some of the things Paul writes in the passage you are about to study. Also compare Philippians 2:8-11.

3. As you study 1:15-23, keep its context in mind. Chart I shows the "next-door neighbors" of the passage.

II. ANALYSIS

Segment to be analyzed: 1:15-23
Paragraph divisions: The study segment of this lesson is essentially one long paragraph. In fact, if you examine the text of your King James Bible, you will note that the entire paragraph is one extended sentence. Modern versions do break up the paragraph into many sentences for easier reading. Regardless of the punctuation used, there is a unifying thought throughout, each clause leading up to the next one until the climactic phrase "all in all" is reached (v. 23).

A. General Analysis

1. Read the passage once or twice, underlining key words and phrases in your Bible as you read. What are some important *repeated* words? Observe for example how many thing are identified as God's by the repeated pronoun "his" (e.g., "his calling," v. 18).

2. What does the opening word, "wherefore" (1:15), refer to?

_____

_____

3. What evidences are there in verses 15 and 16 that Paul had a specific Christian group in mind when he wrote this letter?

_____

_____

4. Observe how the analytical Chart J divides this segment into three main parts. What is Paul's *general* theme in verses 15-18*a*? How is this *particularized* in 18*b*-19*a*?

_____

40

PAUL'S PRAYER	15 MY PRAYERS, that the GOD of our Lord Jesus Christ the FATHER of glory, MAY GIVE UNTO YOU the spirit of wisdom and revelation in the knowledge of him.	GENERALIZATION
3 SPECIFIC PRAYER REQUESTS	18b THAT YE MAY KNOW ① ② ③	PARTICULARIZATION
GOD's POWER	19b according to THE WORKING OF HIS MIGHTY POWER —wrought in Christ when he	
v 20	①	AMPLIFICATION
vv 20-21	②	
v 22a	③	
v 22b	④	
	23	

What point of verse 19*a* is *amplified* in 19*b*-23?

_____

_____

5. Use Chart J as a place to record your observations of this passage. For example, record important phrases of the text inside the main rectangle. (Because so many phrases are strong ones, you may want to record the entire Bible text, similar to the textual recreation of v. 17 shown as an example.)
6. Record on the chart Paul's threefold prayer (1:18*b*-19*a*), introduced by the phrase "that ye may know." This is the strategic center of this passage.
7. Compare the beginning and ending of this segment.

B. Verse Analysis

1. What does verse 15 reveal about the Ephesian Christians?

_____

Compare this verse with these similar references: Romans 1:8; Colossians 1:4; 1 Thessalonians 1:3; 2 Thessalonians 1:3; Philemon 5.
2. What does verse 16 reveal about Paul?

_____

_____

What two ingredients of prayer are cited here?

_____

_____

_____

What is the strength of "cease not"?

_____

_____

3. Read verses 17 and 18*a*. How is God identified here?

_____

What is meant by each phrase of identification?

_____

_____

What common thought is represented by the four words "wisdom," "revelation," "knowledge," and "understanding"?

_____

In your own words, what did Paul want his readers to experience?

_____

Do you think the phrase "eyes of your understanding" refers to mere intellectual knowledge?
4. Read verses 18b-19a. Study the three *specifics* of Paul's prayer request. What is meant by each, and how is the Christian helped by an experiential knowledge of each? Record on Chart K.

PAUL'S PRAYER   **Chart K**

THE RELATIONSHIP	MEANING	VALUE TO THE BELIEVER
The hope of HIS CALLING (PAST)		
The riches of the glory of HIS INHERITANCE (FUTURE)		
The exceeding greatness of HIS POWER (PRESENT)		

5. The first two words of 19b are "according to." This is Paul's "measuring stick" phrase. He has just finished writing of the "exceeding greatness" of God's power in the lives of believers. But he is not content to measure that greatness by the mere word "exceeding," superlative as it is. So he spells out that measurement by some striking examples, showing acts of God that He wrought in Christ. Study verses 20-23 carefully, and record those different ministries on Chart J in the appropriate paragraph box. Which is the key divine work of this list?
6. On the truth of resurrection power in the believer's walk, read Romans 6:4-14; Philippians 3:10; Ephesians 3:20.

43

7. Other important doctrines are taught in verses 19*b*-23. List these below:
Doctrines about Christ

Doctrines about the church

---

8. Compare verses 22 and 23 in a few modern versions. On the last phrase of 1:23, read John 1:16; Ephesians 3:19; 4:10; Colossians 3:11.

II. NOTES

1. "Father of glory" (1:17). A correct paraphrase of this would be: "The Father to whom the glory belongs." The article "the" modifying "glory" is in the original text, putting emphasis on *glory*.

2. "Spirit of wisdom" (1:17). Such a spirit of wisdom is not attainable without the ministry of the Holy Spirit. Read Isaiah 11:2, where the word "spirit" appears four times, once as the person "Spirit." Some prefer to translate all those references as "Spirit."[1]

3. "Eyes of your understanding" (1:18). This could be translated "eyes of your heart." Mere intellectual knowledge is not meant here. "The mind alone cannot grasp the truth of God; the heart of man, his affections and especially his will, must all be bent to the task. Otherwise the essential part of divine revelation will escape the student, leaving only an unsatisfying and incomprehensible framework within his grasp. *In this lies the explanation of much barren intellectual study of Scripture.*"[2]

4. "Hope of his calling" (1:18). Read 1 Thessalonians 5:24 concerning the sure fulfillment of this calling. Among the prospects of this blessed hope is the believer's being conformed to the very image of Christ (Rom. 8:29) to dwell with Him for all eternity.

5. "His inheritance in the saints" (1:18). Christians are God's inheritance—a humbling thought indeed. As one writer puts it,

1 See F F Bruce, *The Epistle to the Ephesians*, p 39.
2 Alexander Ross, "The Pauline Epistles," in *The New Bible Commentary*, p. 1019 (italics added)

"We can scarcely realize what it must mean to God . . . to see creatures of His hand, sinners redeemed by His grace, reflecting His own glory."³

6. "The fulness of him" (1:23). *The Amplified Bible* adds these comments to verse 23: "For in that body [church] lives the full measure of Him Who makes everything complete, and Who fills everything everywhere [with Himself]."

IV. FOR THOUGHT AND DISCUSSION

1. Observe the references to faith, hope, and love in this passage. How does successful Christian living depend on these ingredients? Compare 1 Corinthians 13.

2. It has been said that God's love is best seen in the cross and His power is best demonstrated in the empty tomb. What do the cross and the empty tomb have to do with everyday Christian living?

3. How would you compare heart experiential knowledge and head intellectual knowledge? Since the believer should be growing in the knowledge of Christ, what can he do to help that growth? For some answers to this, study 2 Peter 3:14-18, which is the context of the familiar exhortation "Grow in grace, and in the knowledge of our Lord and Saviour Jesus Christ."

4. What kind of power does the Christian need to live victoriously? Can you identify your own spiritual weaknesses? How does it help to know how mighty one's spiritual resources are? How can one tap those resources?

5. Does the exaltation of Christ, described in 1:20-23, impress you in any way?

V. FURTHER STUDY

1. The word "exceeding" (1:19) translates the Greek *huper* ("beyond") and *ballo* ("throw"). Paul frequently used compound words with this prefix, *huper*. Vincent says that this is "characteristic of Paul's intensity of style, and marks the struggle of language with the immensity of the divine mysteries. . . . "⁴ Paul is the only New Testament writer to use the combination *huperballo*. Study how it is used in these verses: 2 Corinthians 3:10 ("excelleth"); 9:14; Ephesians 2:7; 3:19 ("passeth"—"surpassing").

3. Bruce, p 40
4. Marvin R. Vincent, *Word Studies in the New Testament*, 3:371.

2. Read 1:19 again and observe the similiar terms referring to God's strength. Four different words appear in the original text:

"power" (*dynamis*)   "mighty" *(ischyus)*
"working" *(energeia)*   "power" *(kratos)*

What English words are derived from the first two cited above? What different thought is expressed by each of the four words as they are used in the sentence? Consult an exhaustive concordance[5] and a book on word study[6] for help on the shades of meaning in the words.

VI. WORD TO PONDER

I pray that your hearts will be flooded with light so that you can see something of the future he has called you to share. I want you to realize that God has been made rich because we who are Christ's have been given to him (1:18, *The Living Bible*).

---

5 Two standard works are James Strong, *The Exhaustive Concordance of the Bible*, and Robert Young, *Analytical Concordance to the Bible*.
6. An excellent source book on New Testament words is W E Vine, *An Expository Dictionary of New Testament Words*

Lesson 5

Ephesians 2:1-22

Once Dead, Now Alive

We move now to the second chapter of Ephesians, where the key word is "remember" (2:11). In chapter 1 Paul's appeal and prayer was that his readers might *know* how rich in Christ they really were. Now his appeal is for Christians to *remember* their lost condition before they were saved and to compare this with their life and relationship to God now. The vibrant, cheerful tone of chapter 1 is carried over into this chapter. It is a spiritual tonic for grateful Christians, a rebuke and reviver of the backslidden, and a gospel witness to the unsaved. If you as a Christian entered into the spirit of chapter 1 in praise to God and in seeking to know more fully what you have in Christ, your study of chapter 2 should maintain that momentum and multiply the spiritual blessings already received.

I. PREPARATION FOR STUDY

1. You may want to study this lesson in two or more units since a relatively large amount of text is involved. For example, the passage 2:1-10 could be studied as a complete unit, followed by 2:11-22. Doing this will not jeopardize any continuity of perspective.

2. Review Chart F, observing what chapter 2 contributes to the theme of the epistle. Recall that the emphasis of Ephesians 1–3 is *is our position in Christ*, whereas that of Ephesians 4–6 is *Christ's life in us*. As you study chapter 2 you will want to look for various references to the believer's position in relation to God.

3. Try to imagine how an unsaved Gentile (non-Jew) might react to a gospel witness by a saved Jew in Paul's day, especially since it was a known fact that almost all of the first Christians were Jews, their Scripture was the Jewish Bible, and their Saviour was a Jew. As was noted earlier, most of Paul's readers were Gentile

47

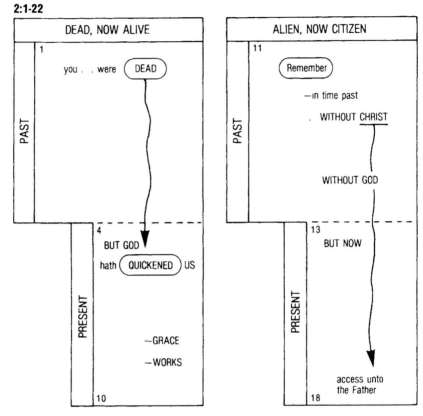

```
┌─────────────────────────────────┐  ┌─────────────────────────────────┐
│         DEAD, NOW ALIVE          │  │        ALIEN, NOW CITIZEN        │
├─┬───────────────────────────────┤  ├─┬───────────────────────────────┤
│ │ 1                             │  │ │ 11                            │
│ │   you . . were   ( DEAD )     │  │ │        ( Remember )           │
│ │                               │  │ │                               │
│P│                               │  │P│      —in time past            │
│A│                               │  │A│      . WITHOUT CHRIST          │
│S│                               │  │S│                               │
│T│                               │  │T│                               │
│ │                               │  │ │        WITHOUT GOD            │
│ │                               │  │ │                               │
├─┴──┬──────────────────────────┤   ├─┴──┬──────────────────────────┤
│    │ 4                         │   │    │ 13                        │
│    │  BUT GOD                  │   │    │  BUT NOW                  │
│    │  hath ( QUICKENED ) US    │   │    │                           │
│  P │                           │   │  P │                           │
│  R │                           │   │  R │                           │
│  E │                           │   │  E │                           │
│  S │   —GRACE                  │   │  S │                           │
│  E │   —WORKS                  │   │  E │        access unto        │
│  N │                           │   │  N │        the Father         │
│  T │ 10                        │   │  T │ 18                        │
└────┴──────────────────────────┘   └────┴──────────────────────────┘

┌─────────────────────────────────────────────────────────────────┐
│                    A HABITATION OF GOD                            │
├───────────────────────────────────────────────────────────────────┤
│ 19            Now therefore                                       │
│                                                                   │
│                                                                   │
│                                                                   │
│ 22                                                                │
└───────────────────────────────────────────────────────────────────┘
```

48

Christians (cf. 2:11; 3:1, 6, 8; 4:17). It is in this second chapter of Ephesians that Paul clearly recognizes an alienation between Jews and Gentiles and shows how the two are brought together in Christ. Read 1 Cor. 10:32, which clearly distinguishes between Jew, Gentile, and the church of God.)

II. ANALYSIS

Segment to be analyzed: 2:1-22
Paragraph divisions: at verses 1, 11, 19

A. General Analysis

1. After you have marked the paragraph divisions in your Bible, read the chapter for early impressions. What is the chapter mainly saying?

---

2. Underline in your Bible key words and phrases.
3. Did you observe in the passage an alternation between the past and present tenses in connection with the believer's experience? Why is "remember" (2:11) a key word?

---

4. Scan the chapter again and note how frequently the text keeps alternating between the pronouns *you* and *we*. When Paul writes "you," he means the Gentile believers. When he writes "we" (or "us"), he means either Jews (e.g., 2:3) or Gentile *and* Jewish believers (e.g., 2:18). You will want to recall this later when you examine the verses more closely.
5. Chart L is a work sheet for recording your observations as you study the paragraphs of this passage. The arrangement of the rectangles shows the basic structure of the chapter. Note the following:
a) The two top areas represent the first two paragraphs (2:1-10 and 2:11-18), which are similar in content. (How does the chart show the two paragraphs to be similar? Does the text support this?)
b) There is a clear break in thought at 2:4 (first paragraph) and 2:13 (second paragraph). Read the Bible text. What is the break in each case?

How is this shown on Chart L?

_c)_ The last paragraph (2:19-22) stands by itself, though it is intimately related to what goes before. How does this paragraph serve as a conclusion to the chapter?

_d)_ Use Chart L to record observations and outlines as you make and develop these in the course of your study.

B. Paragraph Analysis

1. Paragraph 2:1-10: Once Dead, Now Alive
What phrase in 2:1-3 describe the life of the unbeliever before his conversion? What is meant by each phrase? Record below:

	life "in time past"	meaning
v. 1		
v. 2		
v 3		
v. 3		
v. 3		

Why is Satan referred to as "the prince of the power of the air" (2:2)?

What is meant by "children of wrath" (2:3)? (Cf. John 3:36; Rom. 1:18.)

What is the impact of the words "But God" in verse 4?

50

Where does the salvation of a soul originate?

_____

_____

Compare "you . . . who were dead" (2:1) and "God, who is rich in mercy" (2:4). How does verse 4 pick up the main thought introduced in verse 1, after the parenthesis of verses 2 and 3?

_____

What do verses 4-10 teach about the following subjects?
God:

_____

_____

_____

Christ:

_____

_____

_____

Way of salvation:

_____

_____

_____

_____

The new life:

_____

_____

_____

Why is God's grace emphasized in these verses?

_____

_____

Compare the following phrases: (1) "not of works" (2:9), (2) "his workmanship" (2:10), and (3) "unto good works" (2:10).

2. Paragraph 2:11-18: Once Alienated, Now Reconciled

This paragraph is about the two kinds of alienations of Gentiles: (1) from Israel, (2) from God and Christ. Read the paragraph and note the specific references to Gentiles and Israel. Note also the repeated word "both" (also "twain") where the references refer to the two groups, Jew and Gentile. Read the paragraph in a modern version to check your conclusions. What wall separated Jew and Gentile in Paul's day (2:14)?

Observe the different uses of the word "peace" in the paragraph. Compare Isaiah 52:7; 57:19. According to this paragraph, how does Christ bring Jew and Gentile together?

What is the far-reaching significance of this truth when applied universally?

In what sense do unsaved Jews have more light than unsaved Gentiles? (Cf. Rom. 3:1-2; 9:3-5.)

What verses in this paragraph teach the more important truth of a person's reconciliation to God? Compare "But now" (2:13) with "But God" (2:4).

What is the *way* to reconciliation (2:13, 16, 18)?

Is the message of reconciliation the same to all men, whether Jew or Gentile (2:17)?

Here is an interesting outline of 2:13-18:[1]

> Distance done away—"Ye are made nigh"
> Disunion done away—"He hath made both one"
> Division done away—"Broken middle wall"
> Dissension done away—"He abolished enmity"
> Distinction done away—"Of twain one new man"

3. Paragraph 2:19-22: A Habitation of God.

How does verse 19 connect this paragraph to what goes before?
What truths do the following *figures* teach, as they are used by Paul:

"household" (v. 19)

"foundation" (v. 20)

"corner stone" (v. 20)

"building" (v. 21)

"temple" (v. 21)

"habitation" (v. 22)

Compare Peter's use of similar figures in 1 Peter 2:4 ff.
Observe the references to each member of the Trinity in the paragraph.

III. NOTES

1. "By grace are ye saved through faith" (2:8). This is the source text of the Reformation's watchword: *sola gratia, sola fide, soli Deo gloria* ("by grace alone, through faith alone, to God alone by glory"). On the phrase "through faith," Martin writes, "Paul never says *on account of faith,* for faith is not the cause, only the channel through which our salvation comes."[2]

2. "Circumcision" (2:11). This was an Israelite's external sign of participation in the covenant originally made with Abraham, father of the Jewish race (Gen. 17:9-14).

1 J. Sidlow Baxter, *Explore the Book*, 6:174.
2. Alfred Martin, "The Epistle to the Ephesians," in *The Wycliffe Bible Commentary*, p. 1306.

3. "Covenants of promise" (2:12). God's covenants of blessing were originally made to Abraham (Gen. 12:2 ff.; 13:14 ff.; 17:1 ff.; 22:15 ff.) and reaffirmed to Abraham's son, Isaac (Gen. 26:2 ff.), and to Isaac's son Jacob (Gen. 28:13 ff.; 35:9 ff.).

4. "He is our peace, who hath made both one" (2:14). Christ is the great Reconciler of enemies. Bruce writes:

> No iron curtains, color bar, class distinction or national frontier of today is more absolute than the cleavage between Jew and Gentile was in antiquity. The greatest triumph of the gospel in the apostolic age was that it overcame this long-standing estrangement and enabled Jew and Gentile to become truly one in Christ. Those who enter into peace with God must have peace with one another.[']

5. "The middle wall of partition" (2:14). The figure of the wall probably refers to the wall in the Temple area at Jerusalem which separated the Court of the Gentiles from the Court of the Jews. The penalty for a Gentile's entering the Jews' court was death. (Compare Paul's experience recorded in Acts 21:26-29).

6. "Foundation of the apostles and prophets" (2:20). The prophets meant here are the New Testament prophets (cf. 3:5; 4:11). No contradiction is to be seen between this verse and 1 Corinthians 3:11.

7. "Jesus Christ himself being the chief corner stone" (2:20). Consult a Bible dictionary for a description of a cornerstone. "The expressions 'the head of the corner' (Psa. 118:22) and the 'head-stone' (Zech. 4:7) seem to warrant the conclusion that the 'corner stone' is a term equally applicable to the chief stone at the top and that in the foundation."[']

IV. FOR THOUGHT AND DISCUSSION

1. What does it mean to be "dead in trespasses and sins" (2:1)? What happens when God "quickens" us (2:5)?

2. Why should factions and divisions not exist in God's family? In what ways is Christ our Unifer?

3. We are not saved *by* works but *unto* works (2:9-10). What does this mean? How should our lives manifest this vital truth?

4. What is your relation to each Member of the Trinity, as suggested in 2:19-22? How should these relationships affect your daily walk?

---

3 F F. Bruce, *The Epistle to the Ephesians*, p 54
4 Merrill F. Unger, *Unger's Bible Dictionary*, p. 223.

V. FURTHER STUDY

1. Satan is the "prince of the power of the air." Study the doctrine of Satan in the Bible, looking into such questions as to why God has permitted this adversary to have such power (cf. Job 1).

2. Refer to a commentary for further light on 2:21-22. *(The New Bible Commentary* has an interesting treatment of this.)

VI. WORDS TO PONDER

And so the feud ended at last at the cross (2:16*b*, *The Living Bible*).

Lesson 6

Ephesians 3:1-21

Paul's Testimony and Prayer

Chapter 3 is the natural follow-up of chapter 2, as shown by the connective "for this cause" (3:1). In 2:19-22 Paul viewed the saints of the Asian churches as stones placed one by one in the building of God's holy temple to be His glorious habitation throughout all eternity. However, the completion of such a temple project was an event yet future in heaven. So Paul wanted to remind his readers that blessings of that abode were not only of the distant *future* but also of the *today*. This is the theme of his prayer for the saints, which finally appears in the chapter at 3:14-19. Why the prayer is not the very next thing recorded in the chapter is explained below.

I. PREPARATION FOR STUDY

1. One of Paul's famous digressions, or parentheses, appears in this chapter.[1] Refer to the Bible text and observe this sequence:

a) 3:1—Paul begins his prayer with the words "For this cause I Paul, the prisoner of Jesus Christ for you Gentiles."

b) 3:2-13—Paul digresses to write about his ministry to the Gentiles. The word "Gentiles" in the opening breath of his prayer (3:1) brought on this excursion of thought.

c) 3:14-19—Paul resumes his prayer, beginning with the original words, "For this cause I. . . "

2. Paul writes this epistle from a prison in Rome. "I . . . am here in jail because of you—for preaching that you Gentiles are a part of God's house" (3:1, *The Living Bible*). If you trace Paul's steps backward from the Roman jail to when he was first arrested,

---

1. H. C. G. Moule comments that "such tangents and excursions of thought are characteristic of overflowing minds" overwhelmed by the "impulse to diverge into the rich fields beside the road" (*Ephesian Studies*, p. 109).

you will find that his accusers were Jews and that the occasion for the arrest was a false charge about the Jew-Gentile issue. Read Acts 21:18-36 carefully, and you will have an excellent background to Ephesians 3:1-13.

3. Review your earlier studies made of the following words that appear in the text of our present lesson: *dispensation, mystery, heavenly places.*

4. Review Chart F, noting the context of chapter 3.

II. ANALYSIS

Segment to be analyzed: 3:1-21
Paragraph divisions: at verses 1, 14

A. General Analysis

1. Read the entire chapter in one sitting. What are some of your first impressions?

2. What is the tone (atmosphere) of each paragraph?

3. What is the main point of each paragraph?

4. Chart M is a work sheet on which you may record observations as you study. Note the things that are already recorded. The structure of the chapter is clearly laid out on the chart. It is important to see the *whole* of the chapter as you analyze the *parts.*

B. Paragraph Analysis

1. Paragraph 3:1-13: Paul's Testimony of Ministry
Underline in your Bible the various repetitions of these words (include synonyms): *mystery, known, given, Gentiles.*
Go through the paragraph and note everything said about Paul's ministry. (For example, v. 1 gives three such facts.) The word "dispensation," v. 2, means "stewardship." Record below.

_____

_____

_____

_____

_____

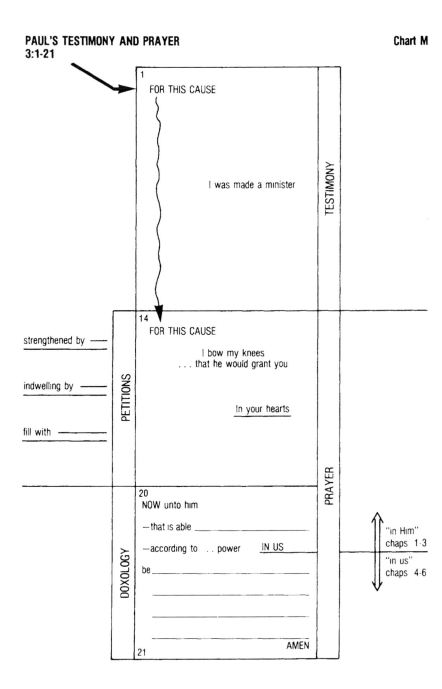

1

FOR THIS CAUSE

I was made a minister

TESTIMONY

14

FOR THIS CAUSE

I bow my knees
. . . that he would grant you

In your hearts

strengthened by ——

indwelling by ——

fill with ——

PETITIONS

20

NOW unto him

— that is able _____

— according to . . power   IN US

be _____

AMEN

21

DOXOLOGY

PRAYER

"in Him"
chaps 1-3

"in us"
chaps 4-6

58

What mystery is Paul writing about in verses 3-6? (See *Notes.*)
Why do you think God withheld revealing that mystery from "sons of men" in the pre-Christian era (3:5)?

_____

_____

Was Paul assured that God had called him to minister primarily to Gentiles? What does Paul say about this in this paragraph?

_____

Read Acts 9:6, 13-16 for the original call to that ministry.
Compare Acts 13:44-49 for an example of Paul's approaches in a typical evangelistic crusade. Read also Romans 15:15-21.
How did Paul relate the following to his ministry:

grace of God (v. 7)   _____

power of God (v. 7)   _____

riches of Christ (v. 8)   _____

wisdom of God (v. 10)   _____

eternal purpose of God (v. 11) _____
How did Paul compare himself with other Christians (3:8; cf. 1 Cor. 15:9; 1 Tim. 1:15)?

_____

_____

Compare verses 9 and 10 as to the following:

	verse 9	verse 10
Who is enlightened?		
About what?		

Who do you think are the "principalities and powers in heavenly places?" (Cf. 6:12.) The phrase "by the church," v. 10, is better translated "through the church" (NASB*).

In verse 12 Paul is referring to access to what (or to whom)?

How does the truth of this verse account for verse 13?

Compare 3:13 and 3:1. Paul has now returned to the place where he got off on a tangent. Hence the next verse (3:14) picks up the original thought (prayer), which he had not even expressed in words as yet.

For a reference to severe tribulations that Paul experienced while ministering in the vicinity of Ephesus just five years before writing Ephesians, read 2 Corinthians 1:8-11.

2. Paragraph 3:14-21: Paul's Prayer for Their Spiritual Growth

Paul can only outline in brief form what he no doubt prayed in solitude for hours and on numerous occasions. Study the prayer not only to learn what daily spiritual experience may be yours, but also to learn how to pray.

Observe on Chart M that the prayer is divided into two main parts: PETITIONS and DOXOLOGY. You will notice, however, that Paul does not write about the petitions until he first tells us how he *approaches* God. What is Paul's heart attitude according to the opening verses of the prayer (3:14-15)?

Why is such an approach necessary?

What is meant by the phrase "the whole family in heaven and earth" (3:15)?

Study carefully the various petitions of Paul. Circle in your Bible the word "that" as it appears three times in verses 16 and 17. (In v.

* *New American Standard Bible*

60

19 the word has a different meaning: "in order that" or "so that"
—Berkeley.) Read the three petitions introduced by this word. Record the various parts of these petitions on Chart

THE THREE PETITIONS OF 3:16-19   **Chart N**

VERSE	SUBJECT	VERB	OBJECT	"with"	"in"	"by"
16	he					
17a	Christ					
17b-	ye	may be able to ①				
19		②				

N. Not all the boxes on the chart will receive an entry.
How are the three Persons of the Trinity referred to here?

_____

If Paul's readers are already Christians, what does he mean by the
prayer "that Christ may dwell in your hearts by faith"?

_____

What is the strength of the word "dwell"?

_____

_____

How does this truth of Christ dwelling *in the believer* anticipate
the practical chapters that are to follow?

_____

_____

Compare also the phrase of 3:20 "the power that worketh *in us.*" How do *faith* (v. 17) and *love* (v. 17) enable Christians to comprehend what Paul writes about in verse 18?

What is your question as you read "breadth, and length, and depth, and height" (3:18)? What is a possible answer? Refer to various Bible versions for suggestions.

Does the word "know" of verse 19 refer to head knowledge or experiential knowledge? What is the blessed fruit of this knowledge of Christ's love (v. 19)?

Translate the last phrase of verse 19 as "filled unto all the fullness of God."
Study the doxology (3:20-21) carefully. It is an intrinsic part of Paul's prayer. Who is the central Person here? What does Paul ascribe to Him?

Compare "able to do" and "that we ask."

What is the strength of the words in between: exceeding, abundantly, above all?

What is Paul's frustration in measuring divine things?

Note Paul's favorite measuring stick: "according to" (3:20). What is God's ability measured here to be?

How does the phrase "that worketh in us" (3:20) refer to the main subject of the next three chapters? See the survey Chart F, where this verse is cited.

How long is "world without end" (3:21)?

What is Paul's heart attitude as he closes his prayer?

How is the doxology a fitting climax to the first three chapters of Ephesians? How is it a realistic "launching pad" for the journey into the final three chapters?

III. NOTES

1. "The mystery" (3:3). Verse 6 states expressly what the mystery is: that Gentile believers would be joined to Jewish believers as fellow heirs, fellow members of Christ's Body, and fellow partakers of His promise. Paul had referred to this earlier in the epistle (e.g., 1:9 ff. and 2:19-22), hence the phrase in 3:3, "as I wrote afore in few words."

2. "Which in other ages was not made known" (3:5). The Old Testament fathers and prophets knew and wrote about salvation for Gentiles (e.g., Isa. 49:6), but the incorporation of Gentile and Jew as fellow members of the one Body of Christ was a mystery not revealed to them.

3. "Now revealed unto his holy apostles and prophets by the Spirit" (3:5). Although this group included others besides writers of New Testament books, the verse does show how writers of the New Testament received divine revelation. Compare 2 Timothy 3:16 and 2 Peter 1:21.

4. "The principalities and powers in heavenly places" (3:10). It is not clear from the text whether only good heavenly beings

are meant here, or good and evil.[2] Martin takes the latter view: "Heavenly beings are observing the Church and seeing in the Church the unfolding of God's wisdom. Both good and evil angels are evidently amazed at the working of God as seen in redeemed men and women."[3]

5. "Manifold wisdom" (3:10). The word translated "manifold" means literally "many-colored."

6. "We have boldness" (3:12). The word "boldness" is derived from two words "all" and "speak" and means literally "to speak freely." (See Further Study.) The basis for such boldness is the object of our faith, Jesus. The last phrase of v. 12 means "through faith *in* Him" (NASB).

7. "Which is your glory" (3:13). Read the verse with this NASB reading: "for they are your glory."

8. "Christ may dwell in your hearts" (3:17). This could be translated "Christ may take His abode in your hearts." *The Living Bible* paraphrases 3:17*a* thus: "And I pray that Christ will be more and more at home in your hearts, living within you as you trust in him."

9. "What is the breadth" (3:18). The text does not expressly state what is the *object* specified by the four dimensions. The following translation identifies this as "the love of Christ" in verse 19:

> With deep roots and firm foundations, may you be strong to grasp, with all God's people, what is the breadth and length and height and depth of the love of Christ, and to know it, though it is beyond knowledge. So may you obtain to fullness of being, the fullness of God himself (*New English Bible*).

10. "Filled with the fulness of God" (3:19). The phrase is better translated "filled unto all the fulness of God." (See Berkeley and NEB* translations.) This suggests a progression of spiritual growing and maturing, as Christ our Indweller accomplishes a divine work in our hearts. An important distinction to make here is that we who are finite cannot *contain* God, who is infinite. But we can *receive* the whole of "those blessings which the Infinite One is willing and able at each moment to bestow upon the finite recipient."[4]

---

2. In 6:12 only evil powers are meant by this same phrase
3 Alfred Martin, "The Epistle to the Ephesians," in *The Wycliffe Bible Commentary*, p. 1308.
* *New English Bible*
4. Quoted in Moule, p 141.

IV. FOR THOUGHT AND DISCUSSION

1. What may have been God's reasons for calling such a strict Jew as Paul to be His minister to Gentiles?[5]

2. What may be learned about humility from Paul's testimony of 3:1-13?

3. It was one of Jesus' disciples who asked this of his Master: "Lord, teach us to pray" (Luke 11:1). What can Christians learn about this vital activity of praying? How can they learn? What does Ephesians 3:14-21 teach about prayer?

4. What does it mean to be "strengthened . . . in the inner man" (3:16)? Have you ever felt weak spiritually? If so, did you find help?

5. What do you think is meant by the phrase "filled with all the fulness of God" (3:19)? Can a Christian know if he is sharing in this blessing?

V. FURTHER STUDY

1. Go back over the first three chapters of Ephesians and compare the various teachings about the Holy Spirit. Note the outline on the Holy Spirit at the bottom of Chart F.

2. Compare the prayer of 3:14-21 with that of 1:15-23.

3. Compare the references to boldness in the following verses: Acts 4:13, 29, 31; 2 Corinthians 7:4; Ephesians 3:12; Philippians 1:20; 1 Timothy 3:13; Hebrews 10:19; 1 John 4:17.

4. Refer to commentaries and other helps for more light on the meaning of these two phrases: "principalities and powers in heavenly places" (3:10); "the whole family in heaven and earth" (3:15).

5. For a review exercise in chapters 1-3, record what *blessings in Christ* are cited in these verses:

1:1 _____

1:3 _____

1:4 _____

1:5 _____

1:6 _____

1:7 _____

1:9 _____

---

5 Read Phil. 3 4-6, where Paul calls himself "an Hebrew of the Hebrews."

1:10 _____

1:11 _____

1:12-13 _____

1:15 _____

1:17 _____

1:18 _____

1:19-20 _____

2:5-6 _____

2:10 _____

2:13 _____

2:21 _____

2:22 _____

3:6 _____

3:10-11 _____

3:12 _____

IV. WORDS TO PONDER

Now glory be to God who . . . is able to do far more than we would ever dare to ask or even dream of—infinitely beyond our highest prayers, desires, thoughts, or hopes (3:20, *The Living Bible*).

Ephesians 4:1-16

Preserving Church Unity

Paul moves down from mountaintop meditations (chaps. 1–3) to practical applications (chaps. 4–6). These are the chapters of the plains and the cities where Christians reveal by their deeds who they really are. The apostle has written much about the Christian's heavenly standing; now he will say some things about the believer's earthly walk. In the first half of Ephesians the emphasis is on the Christian position *in Christ.* Now the spotlight turns on Christ's living *in the Christian.*

Christianity is a life—of real persons called Christians. And Christians are redeemed saints of a real Saviour, Jesus Christ. So doctrines about Christianity and about Christians and about Christ are not cold, lifeless words stored away in a book. They are vibrant truths read and witnessed in the daily walk of believers. As we study the next three chapters of Ephesians we can learn much about how to live the Christian life *today.* This is putting doctrine to practice.

I. PREPARATION FOR STUDY

1. Recall from your survey of Ephesians as a whole that the epistle is mainly of two parts. Chart O, an excerpt of survey Chart F, shows something of the main structure of the epistle. Observe especially where the passage of this lesson, 4:1-16, appears on the chart. What three different areas of a Christian's life are suggested by the outline: Church Unity, Daily Walk, Domestic Duty? Are the three areas intimately related?

2. Read Psalm 68:18, which Paul quotes in Ephesians 4:8. Note that the Psalms reading is "received gifts for men," whereas the

OUR HERITAGE IN CHRIST		THEREFORE →	OUR LIFE IN CHRIST			
WORK OF GOD			WALK OF THE CHRISTIAN			
			CHRISTIAN CONDUCT			
Blessings in Christ	Experience of Salvation	Growing Knowledge and Strength	CHURCH UNITY	DAILY WALK	DOMESTIC DUTY	CHRISTIAN ARMOR
1:1	2:1	3:1	4:1	4:17	5:21	6:10 6:24

THIS LESSON

Ephesians quote is "gave gifts unto men."[1] Actually, in the picture of a conqueror subduing his enemies there is both the receiving of the spoils and tribute from the vanquished *and* the dividing of the spoils to his servants. (Read Ps. 68:12.) It is the latter picture that Paul wants to apply in this Ephesians passage, as we shall see.

3. For background to Ephesians 4:10, read Philippians 2:8-11 and Ephesians 1:20.

4. A quick scanning of the text of chapters 4–6 at this time would be a good general preview of your studies in the remainder of the epistle.

II. ANALYSIS

Segment to be analyzed: 4:1-16
Paragraph divisions: at verses 1, 7, 14[2]

A. General Analysis

1. Read the segment in one sitting after you have marked the paragraph division in your Bible.

1. These two different readings of the Psalms text were in circulation in Paul's day. Refer to a commentary on the problem of this difference. For example, see F.F. Bruce, *The Epistle to the Ephesians*, p. 82.
2. The third paragraph could be studied as beginning at either verse 12, 13, or 14.

(1) THROUGH RIGHT ATTITUDES	ONE GROUP	1
		GOD CALLS
		"one"
(2) THROUGH THE EXERCISE OF GIFTS	VARIOUS GIFTS	7
		CHRIST GIVES
		"gifts"
(3) THROUGH SPEAKING THE TRUTH IN LOVE	HIGH GOAL	14
		"edifying"
		16

2. What is the one prominent subject in each paragraph? (This is clear in the first two paragraphs and not so obvious in the last.) Record your conclusions:
4:1-6

4:7-13

4:14-16

3. Go back over the segment again and underline in your Bible key words and phrases. What are some of the more frequently repeated words?

4. Mark in your Bible each reference to love, Christ, God (the Father), and the Spirit.

5. Chart P is a work sheet for recording your observations, outlines, and interpretations. Study the outline already recorded. You probably have observed many of these in your study thus far.

6. Observe the title on the chart, "Preserving Church Unity." Scan the segment again and note the various references to this unity of believers. Justify the threefold outline on this subject shown in the left-hand column.

B. Paragraph Analysis

1. Paragraph 4:1-6: Right Attitudes
Observe the word "walk" in verse 1. Compare these other appearances of the word in chapters 4-5: 4:17; 5:2, 8, 15. How does this word represent the theme of Ephesians 4-6?

Why does Paul use these words to introduce this new section of his epistle: (1) "therefore" and (2) "I . . . the prisoner of the Lord"?

What is meant by the phrase "walk worthy of the vocation wherewith ye are called"? Compare the reading of various versions. (See Notes.) Is this calling ("vocation") the same for all believers, or is a specialized vocation meant here? Compare Hebrews 3:1; 2 Timothy 1:9.

_____

_____

What attitude of heart should Christians have in their relationships to others (4:2)?

_____

Do you think "one another" (4:2) refers primarily to saints or to all people? Let verse 3 help you in answering this.

_____

Complete this outline for verses 1-3:

v. 1 THE WHAT	v. 2 THE HOW	v. 3 THE PURPOSE

What is the "unity of the Spirit" in a fellowship of believers, such as a local church?

_____

Note the word "keep" in verse 3. This suggests that unity already exists in such a situation. Is it true that a fellowship of believers can originate only when there is harmony among its members? (Note: the words "fellowship" and "communion" translate the same Greek word, *koinonia*, from a root meaning "common," in such verses as Phil. 1:5 and 2 Cor. 6:14.) Why does Paul write "endeavoring to keep" rather than simply "keeping" (4:3)?

_____

_____

What is the key repeated word of verses 4-6? How do these verses support the exhortation of verse 3?

_____

_____

_____

What is the meaning or significance of each of the following seven phrases, as they are used in this context:
a) one body (cf. Col. 3:15)

b) one Spirit (cf. 1 Cor. 12:13)

c) one hope of your calling (cf. 1 John 3:2-3)

d) one Lord (cf. 1 Cor. 8:6)

e) one faith (cf. Jude 3)

f) one baptism (cf. Gal. 3:27)

g) one God and Father of all (cf. 1 Cor. 8:6)

Observing the references to the three Persons of the Trinity in verses 4-6.
Distinguish between each of the following phrases of 4:6:
a) of all

b) above all

c) through all

d) in you all

2. Paragraph 4:7-13: The Exercise of Spiritual Gifts
What is the key repeated word of this paragraph?

Do you see *diversity* in this paragraph? Compare this with the *unity* of the preceding verses. How does verse 13 relate the two?

Compare these readings of 4:7 with the King James Version:

King James Version: "But unto every one of us is given grace according to the measure of the gift of Christ."

Today's English Version: "God gave a special gift to teach one of us, in proportion to what Christ has given."

The Living Bible: "However, Christ has given each of us special abilities—whatever he wants us to have out of his rich storehouse of gifts."

Would it be correct to say that 4:7 states generally for all believers what 4:11 states specifically for certain ones?

Read the paragraph again, and justify this outline:

Gifts for the Christian Ministry
Introduction (4:7)	Specifications (4:11)
Illustration (4:8-10)	Continuing Purposes (4:12)
	Ultimate Purpose (4:13)

Read 4:7. What is this grace?

_____

_____

Read 4:8 (illustration). What is the main phrase of the quotation from Psalm 68:18?

_____

Read 4:9-10. What is the main point of verse 9?

_____

_____

What is the main emphasis of verse 10?

_____

_____

Read 4:11 (specifications). Are all Christians included in this list? (Compare 1 Cor. 12:27-30). In Paul's day, how did each of these minister:

a) Apostles

_____

_____

b) Prophets

_____

_____

73

c) Evangelists

_____

d) Pastors (shepherds) and teachers

_____

Read 4:12 (continuing purposes). What does this verse teach about what the church's functions are?

_____

_____

Read 4:13 (ultimate purpose). What are the three goals mentioned here, introduced by the word "unto?" (Note: The phrase "in the unity" should read "to the unity.")

_____

_____

What is "a perfect man" (4:13)?

_____

What do verses 12 and 13 teach about how church unity is preserved and strengthened through the various spiritual gifts of Christian servants in the church?

_____

_____

3. Paragraph 4:14-16: Speaking the Truth in Love
What words and phrases in 4:14 are in contrast to the word "truth" in 4:15?

_____

Note the two references to love. Why is love included in these two ideas: (1) "speaking the truth in love" (4:15) and (2) "edifying of itself in love" (4:16)?

_____

_____

Compare "grow up" (4:15) and "edifying of itself" (4:16).

Compare "into him" (4:15) and "from whom" (4:16).

What do verses 15 and 16 teach about the unity of believers?

III. NOTES

1. "Worthy (4:1). The word does not express the thought of merit or deserving, but rather that which "becometh" or measures up to. Compare Philippians 1:27 and Romans 16:2, where the same word appears. In Ephesians 4:1, Paul is saying, "Live a life that measures up to . . . " (TEV).

2. "Meekness" (4:2). Christian meekness is not weakness but a composure that is the fruit of power. "It is equanimity of spirit that is neither elated nor cast down, simply because it is not occupied with self at all."³ Jesus said of Himself, "I am meek and lowly in heart" (Matt. 11:29).

3. "One baptism" (4:5). This is the baptism by the Holy Spirit by which a person is put into the Body of Christ. (See 1 Cor. 12:13).

4. "The lower parts of the earth" (4:9). Three different interpretations have been made of this, as to where Christ descended: (1) to Hades (the Old Testament *Sheol*), the abode of the dead (cf. Acts 2:27, where the word "hell" should be translated "hades," and Rom. 10:6-7); (2) to the sepulcher in which Jesus' body was laid; (3) to the earth itself, that is, to this world (cf. John 3:13).

5. "Apostles . . . prophets" (4:11). Apostles and prophets ministered in the churches of the first generation, fulfilling tasks taken over for the most part by the writings of the New Testament (cf. Eph. 2:20). The evangelists (messengers of good news) and pastor-teachers cited in this same verse have continued on in the church's program.

6. "For the perfecting of the saints" (4:12). An accurate translation of 4:12 is the following: "to equip the saints for work of service, for building up of the body of Christ."

---

3 W.E. Vine, *An Expository Dictionary of New Testament Words*, 3.56

7. "The unity of the faith" (4:13). Paul here refers not to "one faith," as in 4:5, but to a unity of Christians that is produced by their common sharing of "the knowledge of the Son of God." Relate the following diagram to 4:13-16:

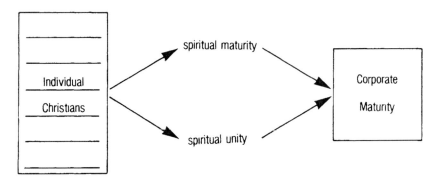

8. "A perfect man" (4:13). This is a mature man. (See a modern version translation.) Read the following verses where this word appears: Hebrews 13:21; 2 Timothy 3:17; James 1:4; 1 Peter 5:10.

IV. FOR THOUGHT AND DISCUSSION

1. How important is unity in a local Christian congregation?
2. Suggest some ways to help preserve church unity, from your own personal experience.
3. Think more about the translation of 4:12 given above (under Notes). Bruce comments on this verse:

> The gifts enumerated in verse 11 do not monopolize the Church's ministry; their function rather is so to help and direct the church that all the members may perform their several ministries for the good of the whole.[4]

It has been said that "in the theocracy of grace there is no laity." In what ways can each member of a local church work in its total program?
4. Is it possible to speak the truth without speaking it in love? If so, what are some examples?
5. Why is truth a key ingredient of Christian unity?
6. What is the usual connotation of the word *ecumenical* as used in the setting of religion today? What is different about that

4. Bruce, p. 86.

kind of "oneness" and the unity about which Paul writes in Ephesians?

V. FURTHER STUDY

1. The subjects of *light* and *love* appear often in the section 4:1–5:20. Make a topical study of this, including the context of each appearance.
2. You may want to refer to various commentaries to learn more about 4:8-10.

VI. WORDS TO PONDER

On him [Christ] the whole body depends. Bonded and knit together by every constituent joint, the whole frame grows through the due activity of each part, and builds itself up in love (4:16, NEB).

Lesson 8

Ephesians 4:17–5:20

The Daily Walk of Christians

The passage of this lesson has much to say about how Christians should behave in everyday living. Many specific commands and exhortations are given, as well as general principles of conduct. Most of the directions involve a Christian's relations to everyone with whom he comes in contact during the course of a day. A few involve just the circle of Christians. As you study the passage, you will become very aware that you are now in the heart of the practical section of Ephesians.

I. PREPARATION FOR STUDY

1. Review your study of last lesson. Recall that the main theme in that preceding passage was the unity of Christians as they grow spiritually in Christ. How does such a theme lead up to the practical specifics of daily living of our present lesson?

CONTEXT OF 4:17—5:20   **Chart Q**

OUR LIFE IN CHRIST					
walk of the Christian					
CHRISTIAN CONDUCT			CHRISTIAN ARMOR		
CHURCH UNITY	DAILY WALK	DOMESTIC DUTY	THE ARMOR	A PERSONAL NOTE	BENE-DICTIONS
4:1	4:17	5:21	6:10	6:21	6:23 6:24

THIS LESSON

78

Chart Q shows the immediate context of the passage we shall now be studying.

2. Read the following Old Testament passage as background to Paul's quotations in the passage: (1) Zechariah 8:16 (see Eph. 4:25); (2) Psalm 4:4 (see Eph. 4:26); and (3) Isaiah 26:19; 51:17; 52:1; 60:1; Malachi 4:2 (only parts of these verses have a likeness to Eph. 5:14).

II. ANALYSIS

Segment to be analyzed: 4:17–5:20
Paragraph divisions: at verses 4:17, 25; 5:3, 6, 15

A. General Analysis

1. First mark the paragraph divisions in your Bible. Observe that we are not making a new paragraph at 5:1. Read 5:1-2 and the verses just preceding them to see a common note here.
2. Read the entire segment in one sitting. What is the main theme of each paragraph? Record below:

4:17-24   _____

4:25–5:2   _____

5:3-5   _____

5:6-14   _____

5:15-20   _____

3. Which paragraphs are mainly about *general* principles of Christian conduct and which are mainly about *specifics* in behavior? Compare your conclusions with those shown in the narrow right-hand column of Chart R.
4. Did you observe any reference to a Christian's relations with another Christian? For example, what may be meant by 4:25b and by this preferred reading of 5:19a: "speaking to one another"?
5. Note the repetitions of the word "talk" in the segment. Complete the outline on Chart R titled HOW CHRISTIANS SHOULD WALK (an example is given).
6. Record on Chart R the key words and phrases that you have observed thus far in your study.

B. Paragraph Analysis

1. Paragraph 4:17-24: The Old Man and the New Man
What is contrasted in this paragraph?

How does Paul relate this to Christian conduct?

Read the phrase "as other Gentiles" (4:17) in line with the pre-ferred reading, "as Gentiles." What does Paul mean by this classifi-cation? (Cf. 2:2).

Read Galatians 1:16; 2:9, where the same Greek word is translated "heathen." Compare also the renderings of Ephesians 4:17 in *Today's English Version* and *The Living Bible.*
Record below at least seven descriptions of unsaved heathen, as given in 4:17-19:

What is the strength of the word "But" in verse 20?

In what sense had the Ephesian Christians heard Jesus and had been taught by Him (4:21)?

HOW CHRISTIANS SHOULD WALK   **Chart R**
4:17—5:20

① WALK AS NEW MEN ___ _____ _____	4 17	GENERAL
② WALK ___ _____ _____	25	SPECIFIC
	5 3	
③ WALK ___ _____ _____	6	GENERAL
④ WALK ___ _____ _____	15	
	20	

81

What is the point of each of these phrases:
a) "put off . . . the old man" (4:22; cf. Rom. 6:6)
b) "be renewed" (4:23)
c) "put on the new man" (4:24; cf. Col. 3:10; Rom. 13:14)
Is it possible to be a new man in Christ Jesus (position) and yet behave like the old man" (experience)?

Is Paul's appeal essentially this: "Be in practice what you are by divine calling"?

How are the "old man" and "new man" described in verses 22 and 24?

How does Paul relate God to "the new man" (4:24).

2. Paragraph 4:25–5:2: The Daily Walk of the New Man
This paragraph answers the question that we might ask at this point, "How should the new man, in Christ, behave among people?" Record on Chart S the many answers Paul gives (an example is given):
What Persons of the Trinity are referred to in the related doctrines noted above?

Read 4:25 again. If "neighbor" refers to saved and unsaved alike, what does Paul mean by "we are members one of another"? (See Notes.)

What are the similarities of 4:28 and 4:29?

Verse	COMMAND OR EXHORTATION		Reason for (or Fruit of) Obeying	Related Doctrines
	negatively stated	positively stated		
4:25	putting away lying	speak . truth with neighbor	for we are members one of another	

List all the truths taught about a Christian's "walk in love" in 4:31–5:2.

_____

_____

_____

_____

How is *truth* (the opening verse of the paragraph) related to *love* (the closing verse of the paragraph)?

_____

_____

3. Paragraph 5:3-5: Appeal to Purity
What different sins are cited in this paragraph?

_____

Note how each of the three lists (one list per verse) ends with a phrase supporting abstinence from the sins cited. What is the force of each phrase in its context?
   "as becometh saints" (5:3*b*)
   "giving of thanks" (5:4*b*)
   "[no] inheritance in the kingdom of Christ and of God" (5:5*b*)
4. Paragraph 5:6-14: Walking as Children of Light
Underline in your Bible the repetitions of the key word, "light."
Observe also contrasting words (e.g., "darkness")
What is spiritual light?

_____

Why is sin not at home in such light? (Apply the illustration of an insect that dwells under a stone and scampers for darkness to hide when the stone is overturned.)
What two groups of people are contrasted in this paragraph?

_____

What is the command to Christians?

_____

_____

What does it mean to be "light in the Lord" (5:8)?

Compare the quote of 5:14.

Based on ancient manuscripts, most modern versions translate 5:9a as "fruit of light" instead of "fruit of the Spirit." How do goodness, righteousness, and truth thrive in light?

5. Paragraph 5:15-20: Walking Carefully
Note the references to the three Persons of the Trinity in the paragraph.
What is meant by these phrases (compare modern versions):
"walk circumspectly" (5:15)

"redeeming the time" (5:16)

"filled with the Spirit" (5:18; cf. 6:18)

Why does Paul use the illustration of wine drunkenness in his appeal for the Spirit's filling? Compare Acts 2:13.

Read the phrase "speaking to yourselves" (5:19) as "speaking to one another" (cf. modern versions). Why does Paul regard thanksgiving as such a vital part of Christian living?

Do you think it is significant that the subject of praise and thanksgiving (5:19-20) follows immediately after the command to be filled with the Spirit (5:18)? Was Paul a good example of a thankful Christian?

_____

_____

Why does Paul include the command about wine in verse 18?

_____

According to this paragraph, what basic heart attitudes are requisites for successful Christian living?

_____

_____

_____

_____

How is the paragraph a strong and positive conclusion to the entire passage on Christian conduct?

_____

_____

III. NOTES

1. "But ye have not so learned Christ" (4:20). "Usually we learn subjects, not persons; but the Christian's choicest lessonbook is his loveworthy Lord. Instruction about Him falls short of the mark; personal intimacy is requisite to rivet the bond of union with the Saviour."[1]

2. "As the truth is in Jesus" (4:21). Bruce writes, "The use of the name Jesus by itself is so rare in the Pauline letters that when it occurs we look for some special significance in it, some emphasis on our Lord's historic incarnation and earthly life. In Jesus, humbling Himself in His real manhood, all truth is embodied."[2]

3. "True holiness" (4:24). The _New American Standard Bible_ translates this as "holiness of the truth." Righteousness and holiness are attributes of truth.

4. "With his neighbor" (4:25). Vine suggests why the New Testament word "neighbour" was very wide in its scope: "There were no farmhouses scattered over the agricultural areas of Pales

---

1. E.K. Simpson and F.F. Bruce, _Commentary on the Epistles to the Ephesians and the Colossians_, p 104.
2   F.F. Bruce, _The Epistle to the Ephesians_, p 93

tine; the populations, gathered in villages, went to and fro to their toil. Hence domestic life was touched at every point by a wide circle of neighborhood."[3]

5. "The devil" (4:27). The word translates *diabolos*, meaning "slanderer." Paul uses the title five times in his epistles, as compared with ten times for "Satan" ("adversary").

6. "An offering and a sacrifice to God for a sweet smelling savour" (5:2). This is an Old Testament picture, teaching that Christ's atoning sacrifice was acceptable to God. Compare Genesis 8:21; Leviticus 1:9, 13, 17.

7. "Be not . . . partakers with them" (5:7). A literal translation is, "Stop becoming fellow partakers with them." This is accentuated in verse 11, "Stop having fellowship."

8. "Redeeming the time" (5:16). A good translation of the entire verse is: "Make good use of every opportunity you get, because these are bad days" (TEV).

9. "Be filled with the Spirit" (5:18). This is not a once-for-all experience. A literal translation is, "Be ye being filled with the Spirit." Martin comments, "A believer can never obtain more of the Holy Spirit, for he indwells the Christian's life in all his fullness. But the Holy Spirit can get more of the believer; that is, he can exercise complete control of the life that is yielded to him."[4]

IV. FOR THOUGHT AND DISCUSSION

1. In your own life, how do you "put on the new man" (4:24)? What makes this even possible?

2. Why does the Bible often follow up a *negative* command with a related *positive* command (e.g., "steal no more . . . rather let him labour")?

3. Can you think of some examples of applying 4:26 to the Christian life? Do the same for 4:27. For the latter, compare 2 Corinthians 2:11 and its context.

4. How is 4:29 represented in this counsel:

Before you speak, ask yourself,

Is it true?	Is it wholesome?
Is it fair?	Will it edify?

5. How does a Christian grieve the Holy Spirit (4:30)? What is the remedy (e.g., 1 John 1:9)?

3 W. E. Vine, *An Expository Dictionary of New Testament Words,* 3.107
4 Alfred Martin, "The Epistle to the Ephesians," in *The Wycliffe Bible Commentary,* p. 1314.

6. What should be a believer's relationship to an unbeliever—at the office, in the neighborhood, at home? Apply 5:7, 11 to this.

V. FURTHER STUDY

The ministry of the Holy Spirit is vital in the daily walk of the believer. After you have read the command of 5:18*b* again, study the following comments carefully:

> No believer in Christ is ever commanded to be indwelt by the Spirit. His indwelling is certain and permanent (Jn 14:16,17). Nor is a believer commanded to be baptized with the Spirit. This has already been done (1 Cor 12.13). But believers are commanded to be filled with the Spirit. Hence there is individual responsibility; there are conditions to be met if we are to experience the Spirit's control in our lives.[5]

What are some of those conditions to be met to maintain the Spirit's filling? (E.g., see 1 Thess. 5:19; Eph. 4:30; Gal. 5:16).

V. WORDS TO PONDER

> And be kind to one another,
> tender-hearted,
> forgiving each other
> JUST AS GOD IN CHRIST ALSO HAS FORGIVEN YOU
> (4:32, NASB, emphasis added)

5. Ibid., p 1313.

Lesson 9

Conduct in the Christian Home

Paul will now have some things to say about Christian conduct and relations in the home. In 4:1-16 his attention was given to the ministry of the church and the unifying relationships of Christians in the work of the gospel. Then his sight was on the everyday walk of believers, whatever contacts they had with other people (4:17–5:20). Now there is one important area yet to be discussed, the home (5:21–6:9). It is not an exaggeration to say that the biggest test of the gospel's transforming power is in the environment of the home. It does not surprise us, therefore, to find Paul's devoting almost the equivalent of one full chapter to this special situation.

I. PREPARATION FOR STUDY

1. Read the following passages whose content is similar to that of the Ephesians passage of this lesson: Colossians 3:18–4:1 and 1 Peter 2:18–3:7. Also, read Paul's epistle to Philemon for what it reveals about the slave-master relationship in Paul's day.

2. If you have access to a Bible dictionary or encyclopedia, read its article on slaves in Bible times. An extensive treatment appears in *Unger's Bible Dictionary* under the title "Service" (pp. 998-99). The following statement taken from that article concerns slaves serving Israelite masters: "Insofar as anything like slavery existed, it was a mild and merciful system, as compared to that of other nations." Read also the footnote to Matthew 13:27, on "slaves," in *The New Berkeley Version*.

3. As you begin your study of this passage, ponder the truth of these words: Each member of the home should be anxious to fulfill his responsibilities before thinking of his rights and privileges.

II. ANALYSIS

Segment to be analyzed: 5:21–6:9
Paragraph divisions: at verses 5:21, 25; 6:1, 4, 5, 9

A. General Analysis

1. Mark the paragraph divisions in your Bible. Why is 5:21 considered here as part of this segment?[1] What general subject does it introduce?

2. What are the six groups mentioned here? (Note: The KJV "servants" of 6:5 is uniformly translated "slaves" in almost all Bible versions.)

In what sense were slaves part of the Christian household?

Are the slaves of 6:5-8 Christians?

3. Make a comparative study of the six groups, recording your findings on Chart T.

B. Paragraph Analysis

1. Paragraph 5:21-24: Wives
What does the phrase "as unto the Lord" add to the basic command of verse 22?

---

1 The close connection between v. 22 and v 21 is supported by the fact that the words "submit yourselves" of v. 22 are not in the original text but are supplied by the translator (shown in italics in most versions) The two verses are joined together thus "Submitting yourselves one to another in the fear of God—wives, unto your own husbands, as unto the Lord "

90

CONDUCT IN THE CHRISTIAN HOUSEHOLD
5:21—6:9

GROUP	MAIN COMMAND	REASONS FOR KEEPING THE COMMAND	CHRIST IN THE COMMAND	RELATED COMMANDS AND EXHORTATIONS	PROMISES AND REWARDS
WIVES 5:22-24					
HUSBANDS 5:25-33					
CHILDREN 6:1-3					
FATHERS 6:4					
SLAVES 6:5-8					
MASTERS 6:9					

Does the word "reverence" of 5:33 add any new thought to what is already expressed by "submit" in 5:22? If so, what?

What is taught here about the relationship of Christ and the church universal (the mystical body of all believers)?

2. Paragraph 5:25-33: Husbands
What is the husband's main obligation to his wife?

How does this compare with the wife's obligation to her husband (5:22)?

What do the following verses teach about the kind of love that a husband owes his wife?
vv. 25-27

vv. 28-30

vv. 31-32

Does Paul suggest by verse 25 that it is even possible for a husband to love his wife with the absolutely perfect love that Christ has for the church? If not, what does Paul intend by this comparison?

What are the implications of the statement, "They two shall be one flesh" (5:31)? Read Genesis 2:20-24.

What does this paragraph teach about the church universal?

3. Paragraph 6:1-3: Children
What do the words "in the Lord" add to the command "obey your parents?"

Compare the meanings of "obey" and "honor."

Read Exodus 20:1-17. Observe what Paul means by "the first commandment with promise" (Eph. 6:2). What is the exact wording of the fifth commandment (Ex. 20:12)?

Since the Ten Commandments were given to the Israelites at Mount Sinai on their journey to the Promised Land of Canaan, what is the specific intent of the phrase of Exodus 20:12, "days . . . long upon the land which the Lord thy God giveth thee"?

Does Paul write Ephesians 6:3 with that same specific application, or does he apply it in a general sense?

4. Paragraph 6:4: Fathers
What is the negative command here? What is the positive command?

Should anything be read into the fact that Paul wrote so little to fathers? In answering this, keep in mind that these fathers were also the husbands of 5:25-33, the longest paragraph of this section. Also, many of these same men were the masters of 6:9.

5. Paragraph 6:5-8: Servants
Are these hired servants Christians?

What commands are directed to such servants?

_____

_____

_____

What motivations are appealed to?

_____

_____

_____

6. Paragraph 6:9: Masters
Observe that no specific command is given here. What does Paul mean by "do the same things unto them"? Compare the reading of modern versions.

_____

_____

_____

What kind of motivation and attitude for masters is exhorted in 6:9?

_____

_____

III. NOTES

1. "Servants [slaves]" (6:5). Paul gives no command in his writings for Christian masters to free their slaves. It is clear that the gospel found slavery firmly established in the world—in many regions a very bad form of slavery. It is natural to inquire into how God approached the problem through His Scriptures. One writer says that God's plan was not to better but to undermine. Stated another way, "The New Testament neither condones the system of slavery, nor demands its immediate and violent overthrow; but it sowed the seeds of many truths, the growth of which would inevitably bring social slavery to an end."[2]

2. "In singleness of your heart" (6:5). The phrase means "with a sincere heart" (TEV). Compare 2 Corinthians 11:3.

_____

2. Alexander Ross, "The Pauline Epistles," in *The New Bible Commentary*, p 1029.

IV. FOR THOUGHT AND DISCUSSION

1. A key thought in this passage is that of submission, or subjection, as introduced by 5:21. Does subordination imply inferiority?

2. What things can fathers do to raise their children "in the nurture and admonition of the Lord" (6:4)? Compare Deuteronomy 6:7.

3. What important lessons may be derived from 6:5-8 as to how Christian employees in this twentieth century can be good witnesses for Christ at their work? Why do many Christians fail to act like Christians at the office or shop? What does this reveal?

4. From your study of this passage, list some important rules for the Christian home that when followed will bring harmony and happiness.

V. FURTHER STUDY

1. Compare the passage of this lesson with the two parallel passages of the New Testament: Colossians 3:18–4:1; 1 Peter 2:18–3:7.

2. Consult outside sources for more light on the New Testament's teaching on slavery.

VI. WORDS TO PONDER

Be submissive to one another out of reverence for Christ (5:21, *Berkeley*).

Lesson 10
Ephesians 6:10–24
The Christian's Armor

Paul's concluding words of his Ephesian letter are among the brightest and most encouraging. He has just finished telling Christians how they ought to conduct their lives, giving them command upon command that must be obeyed if God is to be glorified. Now he speaks as a general to his troops and, pointing to the arsenal of superhuman armor, he assures them of victory if they will but use the divine resources.

The passage of this lesson reveals what we have observed earlier concerning Paul—that he was both a realist and an optimist. As realist, he saw all the spiritual foes of the Christian, arrayed for intense battle (6:12). There was no question in his mind that the Christian conflict is both difficult and dangerous. But the apostle also knew that victory was possible through Christ, hence his vibrant optimism.

I. PREPARATION FOR STUDY

1. Try to visualize Paul in his prison quarters at Rome as he wrote this classic passage on the Christian's armor. There was always a soldier of the guard attending him night and day for more than two years (cf. Acts 28:16). Do you think Paul spoke to those soldiers concerning spiritual matters (cf. Acts 28:30-31)? James Stalker writes these words concerning the armor passage:

> That picture was drawn from the life, from the armor of the soldiers in his room; and perhaps these ringing sentences were first poured into the ears of his warlike auditors before they were transferred to the Epistle in which they have been preserved [1]

1 James Stalker, *The Life of St Paul*, p. 137.

2. Review the survey Chart F to help you recall all that has preceded this concluding passage of the epistle. Note especially the key words that appear along the top of the chart: know, remember, faint not, walk worthily, put on. Chart U is a general overview of chapters 4-6.

CONTEXT OF 6:10-24   **Chart U**

COMMANDS AND EXHORTATIONS				
CHRISTIAN CONDUCT			CHRISTIAN ARMOR	CONCLUSION
CHURCH UNITY	DAILY WALK	DOMESTIC DUTY	THE CONFLICT	
4:1	4:17	5:21	6:10	6:21-24

THIS LESSON

3. The passage of the last lesson was about the Christian home. The present passage is about spiritual warfare. How would you answer this question posed by one unknown writer: "Why so immediately pass from the tranquil duties of home to the very thick of the struggle with assailing spirits?"

4. Refer to a Bible dictionary for a description of the armor of Roman and Greek soldiers in Paul's day.

II. ANALYSIS

Segment to be analyzed: 6:10-24
Paragraph divisions: at verses 10, 14, 18, 21, 23

A. General Analysis

1. Read the whole passage for general impressions. What is the main point of each paragraph:

6:10-13 _____

6:14-17 _____

6:18-20 _____

6:21-22 _____

2. How does the first word, "Finally," identify the function of this last segment of the epistle? What is the last word of the epistle?

_____

_____

B. Paragraph Analysis

1. Paragraph 6:10-13
Which verses of this paragraph contain commands? What are those commands?

_____

_____

What words of the paragraph are about *strength* (cf. 3:16)?

_____

When Paul writes "be strong," does he mean that his readers should acquire new strength or use the strength that is available to them because of their union with Christ?

_____

In what ways are the Christian's enemies identified here?

_____

Who, specifically, are these (v. 12):
a) "principalities" and "powers" (cf. 1:21; 3:10)

_____

b) "rulers of the darkness of this world"

_____

c) "spiritual wickedness in high places"

_____

What phrase in the verse tells us that the above enemies are not individual humans?

_____

What is meant by the two words as they are brought together in verse 13: "withstand . . . stand?" Compare this verse in a modern version.

What is meant by the phrase "whole armour of God"?

How does the Christian put it on (6:11)?

---

2. Paragraph 6:14-17
Does the word "stand" of verse 14 mean the same as the word "stand" of verse 13, as applied to the Christian life?

THE CHRISTIAN'S ARMOR   **Chart V**
6:14-17

ARMOR	SYMBOLIZES	OFFENSIVE OR DEFENSIVE	SOME APPLICATIONS

List on Chart V the various pieces of armor of 6:14-17 and the spiritual weaponry they symbolize.
What different observations, interpretations and applications do you make of this list? For example, why does Paul identify faith as a *shield*? What is the function of a shield?
What is the function of a sword?

Spend much time studying this important practical passage.
3. Paragraph 6:18-20
Do you think Paul considered prayer to be a vital part of the Christian life? Is prayer related to the armor of the previous paragraph?

Do you think Paul had a specific reason in writing about prayer immediately after writing about the Word of God?

For whom does Paul ask intercession (6:18-19)?

What is the reference to Paul's imprisonment in this paragraph? Account for his prayer requests of verses 19 and 20.

---

4. Paragraph 6:21-22
How is this paragraph related to the thought of intercession found in the previous verses?

Compare the two purposes cited in verse 22.

---

5. Paragraph 6:23-24
What five Christian attributes are interwoven in this concluding benediction?

_____

_____

_____

_____

How does this benediction reflect the spirit and purposes of the entire epistle?

_____

_____

_____

III. NOTES

1. "Whole armour" (6:11). The two words translate the one Greek word *panoplia* from which comes our English "panoply."
2. "Spiritual wickedness" (6:12). This is better translated as "spiritual forces of wickedness."
3. "Loins" (6:14). Compare 1 Peter 1:13.
4. "Breastplate of righteousness" (6:14). Compare Isaiah 59:17.
5. "Feet shod with the preparation of the gospel" (6:15). Compare Isaiah 52:7. One way this may be seen as a part of the Christian's armor is suggested by Bruce: "Every Christian should be a bearer of God's good news, and a ready activity in the discharge of this responsibility will be for his own spiritual well-being."[2]
6. "Quench all the fiery darts" (6:16). Fire has always been a formidable weapon in war. Here is a description of one Roman siege in ancient days: "Some advanced with burning torches, others carrying tow and pitch and fire darts, their entire line being illuminated by the blaze."
7. "Sword of the Spirit" (6:17). That is, the sword (God's Word) given by the Spirit. Compare Hebrews 4:12; Revelation 19:13, 15; Hosea 6:5; Isaiah 11:4.
8. "Tychicus" (6:21). Tychichus was no doubt the bearer of this epistle from Paul to the saints in Asia Minor.

2   F.F. Bruce, *The Epistle to the Ephesians*, p. 130

IV. FOR THOUGHT AND DISCUSSION

1. Is a Christian always engaged in a spiritual warfare? If so, in what ways? Weigh the counsel of one unknown writer: "But the ramparts are not for one moment to be left unwatched, nor is the saint ever for a moment to live and move unarmed."

2. If you are studying in a group, discuss fully the armor passage of 6:14-17. This can be an enlightening and heartening experience. Share personal experiences among yourselves to illustrate the truths taught here.

3. What lessons about prayer are taught in 6:18-20?

4. What practical truths are taught in the last two verses of Ephesians?

V. A FINAL THOUGHT

As you conclude your study of Ephesians, think back over the many truths that you have seen and analyzed in the pages of this grand epistle. Let the following brief survey of the epistle help you in recall:

SPIRITUAL WEALTH — PRACTICAL WALK — CONSTANT WAR

Bibliography

COMMENTARIES AND TOPICAL STUDIES

Baxter, J. Sidlow. *Explore the Book*. Vol. 4. Grand Rapids: Zondervan, 1960.

Bruce, F.F. *The Epistle to the Ephesians*. Westwood, N.J.: Revell, 1961.

Foulkes, Francis. *The Epistle of Paul to the Ephesians*. Grand Rapids: Eerdmans, 1963.

Hendricksen, William. *Exposition of Ephesians*. Grand Rapids: Baker, 1967.

Kent, Homer. *Ephesians: The Glory of the Church*. Chicago: Moody, 1971.

Lenski, R.C.H. *St. Paul's Epistle to the Ephesians*. Columbus, Ohio: Wartburg, 1946.

MacArthur, John F., Jr. *Ephesians*. Chicago: Moody, 1986.

Martin, Alfred. "The Epistle to the Ephesians." In *The Wycliffe Bible Commentary*. Edited by Charles F. Pfeiffer and Everett F. Harrison. Chicago: Moody, 1962.

Moule, H.C.G. *Ephesian Studies*. Westwood, N.J.: Revell, n.d.

Ross, Alexander. "The Pauline Epistles." In *The New Bible Commentary*. Edited by F. Davidson, A.M. Stibs, and E.F. Kevan. Grand Rapids: Eerdmans, 1953.

Stalker, James. *The Life of St. Paul*. Westwood, N.J.: Revell, 1912.

RESOURCES FOR FURTHER STUDY

Everyday Bible. New Testament Study Edition. Minneapolis: World Wide, 1988.

Hiebert, D. Edmond. *An Introduction to the Pauline Epistles*. Chicago: Moody, 1954.

Jensen, Irving L. *Independent Bible Study*. Chicago: Moody, 1963.
        . *Jensen's Survey of the New Testament*. Chicago: Moody, 1981.
        . *Prison Epistles*. Do-it-yourself Bible Studies. San Bernardino: Here's Life, 1987.
New International Version Study Bible. Grand Rapids: Zondervan, 1985.
Ryrie Study Bible. Chicago: Moody, 1985.
Strong, James. *The Exhaustive Concordance of the Bible*. New York: Abingdon, 1890.
Unger, Merrill F. *New Unger's Bible Dictionary*. Chicago: Moody, 1966.
Vincent, Marvin R. *Word Studies in the New Testament*. Vol. 3. Grand Rapids: Eerdmans, 1946.
Vine, W.E. *An Expository Dictionary of New Testament Words*. Westwood, N.J.: Revell, 1961.
Young, Robert. *Analytical Concordance to the Bible*. Grand Rapids: Eerdmans, n.d.

Moody Press, a ministry of the Moody Bible Institute,
is designed for education, evangelization, and edification
If we may assist you in knowing more about Christ
and the Christian life, please write us without obligation.
Moody Press, c/o MLM, Chicago, Illinois 60610

CPSIA information can be obtained
at www.ICGtesting.com
Printed in the USA
FFOW05n1527240914

9 780802 444547